THE 1718 COVERLET

Susan Briscoe

THE 1718 COVERLET

69 Quilt Blocks from the Oldest Dated British Patchwork Coverlet

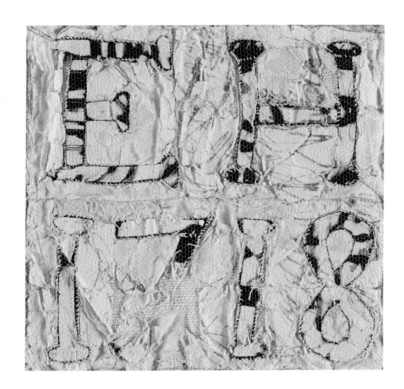

Susan Briscoe

David and Charles

www.stitchcraftcreate.co.uk

The replica of the 1718 Silk Patchwork Coverlet, made by members of The Quilters' Guild of the British Isles. The replica was begun late in 2001 and completed in 2004.

Contents

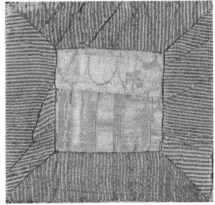

Foreword

Gazing at this wonderful object I get the impression of a sunny day at the end of summer. Washes of leafy greens and earthy browns are shot through with golden light, from creamy off-whites through buttery-yellows to warm honeysuckles and ochres. Then the bold geometric layout strikes me. Hearts, diamonds, circles and crosses surround and mirror image themselves, giving a secure optimism to the whole arrangement; and then the unique features of swans, tulips and fleur-de-lys delight my eye. I am in the midst of a joyous pageant with fluttering silk banners, costumed dancers and music. Because the fabric colours have an uneven, painterly texture, sometimes stripes or brocades, the simplest forms have movement and grace. This is also due in large part to wonderful combinations of colours, the occasional sharp contrast, but mostly softer combinations like blue and golden brown or coral red and ochre. Some of the darkest patches have crumbled leaving a pale surface with only fragments of dark, adding a glow to the piece. Four black squares on point punctuate the outer centre panel, creating a contrast to the warm softness of the overall palette.

It is a patchwork like this that sets the colour mood for most of my quilt designs. I usually go for bright palettes with lots of harmonious combinations of colour. When the shapes in my blocks are bold and simple I can use closer tones that almost lose the structure. When I employ smaller details I have a sharper contrast to my colours but these old patchworks have shown that shades that create a glow are more to my liking than harsh, banging dissidence. To make one's palette optimistic with a child-like freshness, yet in a tone that is ageless, is the inspiration I take from this coverlet. I have seen it countless times over the years and it always draws me into its celebration of colour and jaunty form.

Kaffe Fassett

© The Quilters' Guild of the British Isles

Kaffe Fassett by the Chevron Strippy from The Quilters' Guild Collection at the Quilt Musuem and Gallery.

Details from the 1718 Silk Patchwork Coverlet.

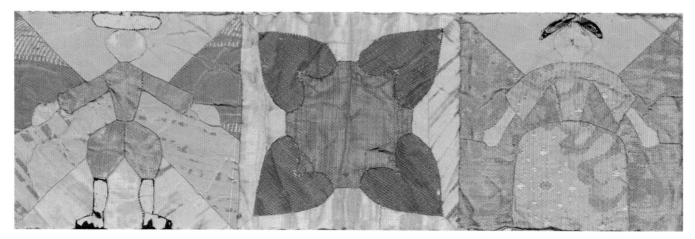

Introduction

This book has been inspired by the 1718 Silk Patchwork Coverlet, which is the oldest known dated piece of patchwork in the British Isles. My hope is that you will also be inspired to create your own replica coverlet, exploring the techniques used in past centuries, or using the modern techniques also described within the book, to create your own version of the coverlet or other smaller projects. The extensive Block Directory in the second half of the book describes how to make all of the blocks in the coverlet.

Dated works, especially early pieces are, according to quilt historians Tina Fenwick Smith and Dorothy Osler, 'priceless because they represent precise points in a quilting time-line that, for the 18th century, especially the early part, is still somewhat opaque'. Surviving textiles from this period are rare. What gives the 1718 coverlet a greater level of interest for quilters today is its marvellous collection of decorative and charming designs, which just beg to be the inspiration for many contemporary reinterpretations. It is a sampler quilt from another age.

There are 182 blocks from sixty-nine different patterns, made from an astonishing array of 17th and early 18th century fabrics, mainly silk. The originals vary between 4½in (11.4cm) for most blocks and 13½in (34.3cm) for the largest designs. They include everything from simple and not-so-simple geometric blocks still used by quilters today to figurative blocks – with everything from hearts and flowers to animals and heraldic devices, even a man and a woman dressed in the fashions of the day. The visual vocabulary has similar elements to 17th and 18th century embroideries, such as samplers and stumpwork boxes, while the charming variety and piecing challenges they bring will whet the creative appetite of the contemporary stitcher.

The coverlet was bought at auction in 2000 by The Quilters' Guild of the British Isles, an educational charity and the UK's national quilt guild. Little of its history was known at that time. Historical research by members of the British Quilt Study Group and a conservation programme were begun almost immediately, but it also inspired the creation of a full-size replica coverlet, which was completed in 2004.

The replica, coordinated by Pauline Adams with Tina Fenwick Smith, aimed to recreate the coverlet in its original colours, before the ravages of nearly 300 years had mellowed its dyes, using the same techniques with the closest modern equivalents of the original silk fabrics, many hand dyed for the project. The replica project archive has formed the starting point for this book. I interviewed Pauline Adams about the replica project, so you can benefit from her experiences, tips and ideas. Quilt historian Bridget Long has also contributed a fascinating chapter about the coverlet's history.

The coverlet maker's technique, mosaic patchwork (also called English paper piecing) with the papers left inside the patchwork as an extra stabilizing layer, may not appeal so much to quilters today, so I have included instructions to enable you to reinterpret the blocks using either the original method or modern patchwork and appliqué techniques. Each block has full-size patchwork and appliqué templates.

The original 1718 coverlet is now very frail despite conservation and its delicate condition means it cannot be displayed often and risk further light damage. To preserve it, it must be kept in the dark in humidity-controlled storage and it is rarely exhibited. We still don't know who made the coverlet and perhaps we never will. One of the best ways we can enjoy it is through this book, and you can continue its legacy by making your own version of the blocks or make smaller projects using your favourite patterns.

We live in a world remote from the coverlet's maker – someone who lived before the industrial and agricultural revolutions that shaped our international world, before electricity and modern communications, who couldn't shop for fabrics as we can, or travel 200 miles in a day to visit a quilt show. But we may have more in common with her through our patchwork than most other aspects of our lives. After all, if we were to meet through a time warp, we could share our passion for patchwork!

Susan Briscoe

A History of the 1718 Coverlet

A short history of the 1718 coverlet by Bridget Long

The timing of the purchase at auction of the 1718 Silk Patchwork Coverlet in the autumn of 2000 could be regarded as perfect. It was acquired by The Quilters' Guild of the British Isles for the Guild's quilt collection at a time when there was a growing interest in the heritage of quiltmaking in Britain. As one of the treaasures of The Quilters' Guild collection, the coverlet inspires, but also intrigues. The last quarter of the 20th century saw a revival of the combined crafts of quilting, patchwork and appliqué, which were 'discovered' by a new generation of textile artists and needlewomen, who also began to appreciate the long history of British quiltmaking.

Detail of 1718 Silk Patchwork Coverlet, showing the initials EH (presumed to be the maker) and the date 1718.

This appreciation was fostered to a great extent by the British Quilt Heritage Project, when over 4,000 objects were recorded during a three-year period, a number of influential British quilt history books were published, including the project book *Quilt Treasures* (see Bibliography) and successful museum exhibitions took place, including North Country Quilts, which was staged at The Bowes Museum earlier in 2000.

In 1998, an inaugural quilt study day led to the founding of the British Quilt Study Group and the research papers from the event were published a year later in the Group's journal, *Quilt Studies*. Now quilt historians had access to a British journal dedicated to the publication of quilt research and read by an international audience. The journal offered an opportunity for various research methodologies to be explored and recorded and it would provide a significant vehicle for an in-depth study of the 1718 Silk Patchwork Coverlet. The 2003 *Quilt Studies* was entirely devoted to this.

The 1718 coverlet is the earliest known British patchwork that has a date worked into the piece, and as such can be used as a benchmark against which all other rare survivors of early 18th-century patchwork can be compared. The international significance of the piece justified a close examination of its likely provenance, design, construction and fabric content, in order to better understand the cultural and social contexts relating to

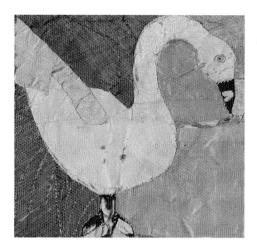

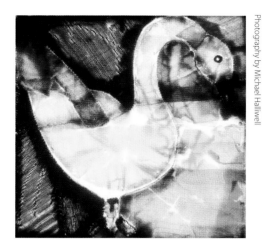

Detail of the 1718 Silk Patchwork Coverlet showing the swan block in Pattern 62 (original blocks 160 and 162).

A transmitted light image of the papers in the swan revealing an earlier draft of the design. In this type of photography a light source is transmitted through the subject toward the lens, revealing details and structures that are often unseen.

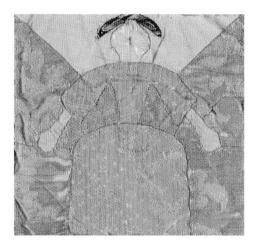

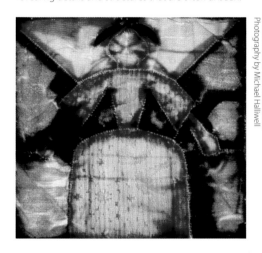

Detail of the 1718 Silk Patchwork Coverlet showing the lady in Pattern 34 (original block 62).

A transmitted light image of the papers in the lady showing the first draft of the design where the skirt was narrower.

the making of patchwork in the century. Patchwork as a term was embedded in the language of the period and was used regularly as a metaphor in political and artistic discourse, but the material and documentary evidence for patchwork practice at this time is more obscure. Importantly, the connections between the practice in Britain and colonial North America had not been examined closely.

The study of the coverlet in an issue of *Quilt Studies*, which was devoted entirely to the research, was groundbreaking in that it demonstrated the variety of ways in which quilt study can be undertaken, and drew on the experience and knowledge of many contributing researchers. The wealth of detailed information from the study has contributed greatly to our knowledge of 18th-century quiltmaking and has prompted further discoveries over the last ten years.

The coverlet was purchased from the Browns of Aldbourne, Wiltshire, a gentry farming family that has been established in north Wiltshire since at least the 17th century. Detailed family history research has failed to identify the maker or the owner of the initials EH, which are featured above the date in the centre of the coverlet, but the unidentified needlewoman stitched the coverlet at a time when there was a fashion for patchwork amongst the higher levels of British society. Thomas Baker, in the prologue to his play *Hampstead Heath* [1] (see back of book for references) of 1706, said that, 'Patchwork is the Fashion of this Age'. Mrs Jane Barker introduces her 1723 novel *The Patch-Work Screen for the Ladies or, Love and Virtue*, saying of patchwork, 'the uncommonness of any Fashion, renders it acceptable to the Ladies. And I do not know but this may have been the chief Reason why our Ladies, in this latter Age, have pleas'd themselves with this sort of Entertainment'.

The maker of the coverlet undertook a testing project to construct a mosaic patchwork [2] design of square and rectangular blocks of varying sizes, from 4½in (11.4cm) square upwards to 13½in (34.3cm), containing geometric or figurative patterns including animals, birds and flowers. Mosaic patchwork is a time-consuming method requiring the use of paper for templates. Made from linen and cotton rags, paper was a valuable commodity at this time and its use in a needlework project demonstrates that the maker could afford to 'waste' paper for her sewing project.

No other silk patchwork object from the 18th century has such a complex design containing both geometric and figurative motifs, but many of the other pieces also have designs based on the square patchwork block, often containing half-square triangular pieces. Most of the surviving objects have been constructed using the mosaic patchwork technique and, for the first time, the conclusion was reached that this patchwork technique can be regarded as an indicator of social class in the 18th century. Surviving late 18th-century examples from North America also show the use of this technique and the continuous use of the technique has been recorded there until, at least, the late 19th century.

The inspiration for the figurative patterns is likely to have been influenced by the genre of sampler making with which the maker would have been familiar, and by focusing on images of household pets, farmyard animals and varieties of game, the maker of the 1718 patchwork coverlet positioned herself within her home and her familiar rural countryside.

Pattern 22 (original block 45) is an example of a 4½in (11.4cm) square block from the original coverlet, while Pattern 63 (original block 175) is an example of a 13½in (34.3cm) square block.

The figurative motifs have a naïve quality about them, but that may be as much a compromise to allow for the degree of difficulty of the patchwork as it is an indication that the maker lacked drawing skills. Some designs in the small blocks incorporate very small paper shapes, requiring skill to wrap with fabric and to manipulate whilst sewing. It would appear that the needlewoman was fully experienced in the patchwork technique, confident in her sewing ability and had free leisure time at home to spend on the work.

The two-year period of study of the 1718 coverlet allowed a detailed analysis of the fabric content. This enabled the researcher to develop a picture of the environment in which the object was made, together with an assessment of the possible sources of the materials, and demonstrated the value of textile analysis to the development of quilt research.

The coverlet is made almost completely from silks with over 120 different designs, mostly plain or simple weaves but also some damasks and brocades containing metal strips of silver. The fabrics are consistent with the social class of the family being relatively high status, but not 'the best fabrics of the day'. [3] Many of the fabrics show evidence of previous use and some are thought to be from the 17th century, demonstrating some recycling of cloth within the household, which was common in the period. Swift, in his *Directions to Servants in General* (published after his death in 1745 but begun over twenty-eight years before), told waiting maids that they can no longer profit from their employment by benefiting from the gift of cast-off dresses, which had a value on the second-hand market. Their 'Comforts and Profits' had been lessened by 'that execrable Custom got among Ladies,… of turning them to cover easy Chairs, or making them into Patch-work for Skreens, Stools, Cushions, and the like'. [4]

Given that so many designs have been recorded in the silks, it is very likely that some of the pieces were obtained from sources outside the home. A number of references to the purchase of patchwork pieces have been recorded throughout the century. Mary Rich was indicted at the Old Bailey court [5] in 1726 for stealing goods including '80 Pieces of Silk value 9s. - 9 Pieces of Brocade Silk, 2s. 6d.', which were described as 'such as were used for Patchwork &c.'.

The paper templates still remain in the coverlet and provide tantalising glimpses of printed and handwritten text. The researchers moved beyond the traditional research techniques to explore ways in which the details of the texts could be read without affecting the condition of the entire coverlet. Soft x-ray analysis was carried out on certain sections of the coverlet in an attempt to decipher some of the handwritten papers, but the results were inconclusive.

Following the conservation of the coverlet, a research project was set up at the Textile Conservation Centre in Winchester to examine the use of photographic techniques to uncover the printed and written marks on the templates. After an initial test using transmitted light photography [6] proved promising, a full photographic record of the papers was created using the technique. This revealed letters, bills

and printed text, as well as fascinating details of the design process and the preparations for the making of the coverlet.

The research has revealed the time the maker spent designing the simpler geometric patterns by folding squares of paper and creating the more complicated geometric and figurative designs by drawing and in some cases, re-drafting on paper squares. Before cutting the paper apart to create patchwork templates, the needlewoman drew lines, numbers and symbols on the shapes to create lining-up marks and guides to ensure that the wrapped patches were joined together in the correct sequence. A lining-up mark that runs across the edge of adjacent templates from two separate blocks, indicates that the maker planned the layout of the patchwork blocks before she started her project.

Pattern 9 (original block 16) is an example of a geometric block from the coverlet.

The serendipitous discovery of a previously un-documented, early patchwork coverlet in 2000 has had a significant effect on the growth of interest in British quilt history. The results of the 1718 coverlet case study have prompted historians to re-appraise the material and documentary evidence for patchwork practice in the 18th century and to expand the knowledge of quiltmaking in the period. Significantly, it has added greatly to the debate concerning the migration of British quiltmaking techniques to English-speaking countries in North America and Australasia over the last 300 years.

The Coverlet and The Quilters' Guild Collection

An article by Heather Audin (Curator of The Quilters' Guild Collection)

The 1718 Silk Patchwork Coverlet is the most iconic item in The Quilters' Guild Collection. As the earliest known initialled and dated British patchwork coverlet, it provides an important dating benchmark for other textiles, and can tell us a great deal about the development of patchwork and quilting in Britain when placed in the context of other historical samples from the 17th and 18th centuries.

The coverlet is one of a handful of items surviving from the early 18th century and is an important representation of the style of patchwork being produced at this time. The Quilters' Guild Collection itself contains over 800 examples of patchwork, quilting and appliqué, which range in date from the early 18th century to contemporary 21st-century quilt art. The aim of the Collection is to represent a varied sample record of the different types and styles of patchwork and quilting over the past three centuries, from varied social classes and historical contexts.

Like most textiles that are several centuries old, the silks in the 1718 patchwork coverlet have been subject to deterioration. Some pieces, notably the black silks, have completely disintegrated leaving only the surviving paper templates behind. The coverlet underwent conservation at the Textile Conservation Centre in Winchester in 2003, to make it safe for long-term preservation and occasional short-term display. It was surface cleaned with a low powered vacuum and the creased areas were relaxed and re-shaped using an ultra-sonic humidifier. The whole

The replica 1718 silk patchwork coverlet on display in 2013 during the 'It's All in the Making' Exhibition at the Quilt Museum and Gallery in York, UK.

This highly magnified detail of Pattern 17 (original block 38) shows how the monofilament netting blends in completely with the paler fabrics, while being unobtrusive against darker silks.

surface was covered with a specially dyed nylon net, which was stitched down with polyester Stabiltex threads around existing stitch lines. This very fine net is difficult to see even on some of the highly magnified images in the Block Directory of this book, and to the naked eye it blends perfectly with the original fabrics, providing stability without significantly altering the look of the original piece.

The coverlet is stored in a humidity controlled and environmentally monitored environment, which is the case for all of The Quilters' Guild Collection. It is rolled on a wide diameter tube with the front facing out and interleaved with acid-free tissue paper. The whole roll is covered in Tyvek, a synthetic material made from high density polythene fibres. It is intended that these measures will preserve the coverlet for future generations to enjoy.

Making your own version of the coverlet, or smaller projects using the blocks, will give you an opportunity to explore its complex visual vocabulary and absorb its fascinating designs into your own block repertoire.

Conservation using monofilament netting on a damaged area of printed cotton on a coverlet from The Quilters' Guild Collection.

© The Quilters' Guild Photography by Catherine Candlin

Making the Replica Coverlet

An interview with Pauline Adams, replica organizer

You may be thinking that the 1718 Silk Patchwork Coverlet would make an ideal group quilt and you would be right. Soon after The Guild bought it, plans were made to create a replica patchwork. This project, begun in November 2001 and completed in 2004, was separate from the study and dating aspects of the research, though these played a helpful part at times. Pauline Adams organized this massive group project and in my interview here she describes how it was done, with many helpful tips for making a version of the coverlet with your quilt group.

SB: Recreating a modern copy of the 1718 coverlet by hand seems like a lot of work. Why did you go to so much trouble to make it as a replica rather than using modern patchwork and appliqué techniques?

PA: Although the original patchwork is in remarkably good condition for its age, it is not robust enough to be displayed very often. It must not be subjected to bright light, camera flashes or touching and handling, so it would be very vulnerable whilst on display, in even the most carefully stewarded venue. Many museums get over this problem by making facsimiles or copies as exact as possible of their most precious or fragile objects – think of the Sutton Hoo treasures – or those they wish to display in two places at once. A facsimile can also help people understand what an item would have looked like new, giving a much better sense of the period than the original alone. This is what we wanted to do with the coverlet.

Is it important enough for all this trouble? The short answer is – yes! This is the earliest known patchwork piece, initialled and dated, anywhere in Britain, so far as is known. It contains magnificent silk fabrics with some traditional but now unfamiliar patterns and some unusual methods of construction, with considerable skill in pattern and colour arrangement, and a refreshing naivety in the patterns used.

SB: So it was a big project to take on – how did you start?

PA: The first decision was to copy it as closely as possible to its original state and also to use materials as similar as possible to the original. First, we assessed the design layout of the coverlet – generally symmetrical about a vertical centre line, so one half mirrors the other. The blocks aren't all exactly the same size, but after much calculation it was decided to make our replica blocks 11cm (about 4½in) square, as we thought this was the nearest whole, practicable measurement. The coverlet is fifteen blocks across and seventeen blocks down. This would be 255 blocks, but because some of them are

larger there are actually only 182 blocks, and most of these have repeats or mirror images. In fact there are sixty-nine completely different block designs. It probably measured 67½in x 76½in (171.5cm x 194.5cm) originally, as the smaller blocks would have been two 'nails' square when made (a nail is 2¼in). I see you've used 4½in (11.4cm) for the standard blocks in this book, which makes the geometric blocks easier for modern patchwork techniques and rotary cutting.

Tina Fenwick-Smith was guardian of the coverlet – long before the Quilt Museum and Gallery opened. I lived over 100 miles away and visited frequently, but a lot of research was done collaboratively by letter and phone, with me asking the questions and Tina looking for answers.

SB: Keeping track of all the blocks must have been difficult in such a big project. How did you plan it?

PA: Tina drew a numbered grid of the blocks, noting any 'specials', like velvet, lettering, animals, birds and so on. This was used as the basis for charting the patchwork patterns and fabrics appearing in each block. The block designs fell into two categories: totally geometric patterns, and geometric patterns onto which detailed patchwork images of animals, birds, flowers and so on were inlaid. I drew out all the blocks. Of course, these steps are already done for you in this book – if you wish to make another replica patchwork – but drawing and numbering a grid is a good way to start adapting the blocks for your own projects, so you know which blocks will go where and how many to make of each design.

SB: Tina's grid has been very useful in preparing the book too – we've used her system to give each block a unique identification number, in addition to the pattern numbers we used for each different, but repeated block. With so many interesting blocks and figurative designs in the patchwork to copy, were you able to trace the patterns directly from the original?

PA: The pictorial blocks were difficult to do because we couldn't touch the coverlet, and direct tracing was totally out of the question. Sketching wasn't sufficiently accurate either. It was photographed laid out flat, without flash, covering the whole area, so I started a system of selecting the right photograph, scanning it – straightening it if necessary – before repeated steps of enlargement and cropping to get the block image to an exact 11cm (4⁵⁄₁₆in). This was printed and the print traced in ink onto an 11cm square drawn on tracing paper. The image was labelled with the number of the block it applied to, then put on a light table and traced in pencil onto another square of acid-free paper for the templates. The geometric patchwork blocks were easier to draft using a parallel motion drawing board, set square, ruler and pencil. Each piece in the block was numbered on the back, with arrows to show the direction of any stripes and balance marks drawn across seam lines to help line up the patchwork pieces.

SB: The technique is what we now call 'mosaic patchwork' and I have included instructions in the Techniques section of this book, based on those you wrote for the project kits. Many of the figurative blocks look like they would be easier to do in appliqué, and I think that's how many readers will probably want to make them today.

PA: We were making a replica, but of course you could use appliqué and machine patchwork for a contemporary version. You would expect the complicated animal, bird, flower and figure blocks to be appliqué, but they were all sewn 'over papers' in the original – each tiny little piece. The figures were generally superimposed on a four-triangle block, or rather

cut out of the middle of the folded paper, which was then cut on the folds to make a frame to the figure. The original was made in blocks by mosaic patchwork, but the papers were left in place, with the tacking (basting) only going through the seam allowance and paper so none of the linen tacking stitches showed on the front. The papers were always intended to be left in the patchwork for stability. This 18th-century technique is recorded by Averil Colby in her book *Patchwork*. Of course, we had to use the same technique for the replica.

Some of the blocks are patchwork patterns that we still know today, now called four-patch, nine-patch and so on, or divided diagonally into four triangles or have an attic window format, although we don't know what the original maker called the designs. Her patchwork patterns were made by folding paper squares in various ways, and then cutting on the appropriate fold lines. Where these folds were left uncut, they have remained as ridges or valleys and unfortunately have worn out the silk over the ridges.

On each of the three heart-star blocks, some of the biggest blocks – which we nicknamed the 'lollipop hearts stars'– the maker actually stitched two pieces of paper together to make a square large enough for the whole 13½in (34.3cm) block. On all three of these blocks, traces of the extra thickness of paper can be seen, and on one block, on the far left of the original, one of the paper pieces has been sewn into the wrong position!

SB: So can you describe what the construction of the original coverlet is exactly?

PA: Each block would have been made in turn, the pieces first being tacked (basted) and then oversewn together. It is likely that when all had been made they would have had a final laying out and swapping around before being stitched together. All this sewing was done with a fine linen thread. A heavier linen thread was used for quilting between the blocks, with the papers left in place. This was obviously intended from the start because of the invisible tacking. Sewing was fifteen to twenty stitches to the inch. Once the top was made, it was backed with old pieces of linen seamed together, and two of these had embroidered initials. We used the same techniques for our replica.

SB: Making up each block as a kit for your stitching volunteers must have been a big part of getting the project started. How many volunteers took part?

PA: It was decided to involve as many Guild members as possible, so kits had to be made up with everything needed, including the silk fabrics. This was an opportunity for members to show their sewing skills, too. Over 200 were people involved, including some who helped with the final assembly at The Guild Conference and AGM weekend but didn't log their names. Mosaic patchwork is a good technique for a large group, because the tacked-in templates mean there's little margin for error, as there can be when everyone is sewing a slightly different ¼in (6mm) seam by machine.

SB: Was it difficult to keep things organized? Any group project needs carefully coordinated fabrics, so what did you include in the kits?

PA: A very fat ledger has kept track of all the blocks and makers! We had to source fine linen thread and acid-free paper for the kits. First we tried Zerkall, a smooth, white 145gsm paper, but Tina felt that this was thicker and stiffer than the papers in the coverlet. We tried another but it had a very soft surface and was difficult to draw on. Later, the first stitchers on the project reported that it was too soft to hold an edge when making tiny complex shapes, so the more complex and larger blocks were redrawn on Zerkall.

The fabrics, paper pattern, sufficient lengths of thread (a two-ply lace thread for tacking and sewing, measured in 20in (50cm) lengths) and a return address label were put into a numbered, resealable plastic bag for each kit. I drafted and printed explanatory notes and instruction sheets. These were personalized for each block and included a thumbnail photo of the block, an A4 copy of a good photograph of the whole coverlet, with a copy of the block diagram and of the whole quilt with the block highlighted on the back. Additional instructions for the difficult blocks, those with curves, were prepared later and added to the kits where needed (see example drawings below). The small block kit fitted into an A4 envelope. The larger blocks had padded envelopes to prevent the paper pattern from being folded and creased in the post. The instruction sheets and the large picture of each block supplied with the kit were for each maker to keep as a souvenir.

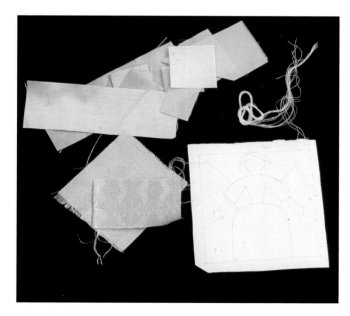

Example of the replica kit supplied to Quilters' Guild members.

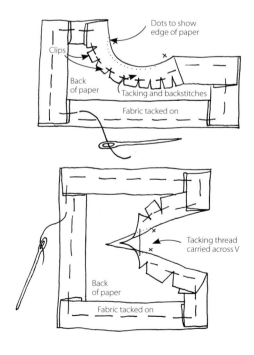

Examples of Pauline's drawings, included in the kits supplied to Guild members making the replica coverlet.

SB: How did you go about finding all the right fabrics? Quilters working today can match the 1718 colours with plains and shot cottons, but matching 300 year-old silks must have been almost impossible!

PA: It was difficult because the original silks were all dyed with natural dyes, and many were woven textures, stripes, brocades or damasks; there was also velvet and some ribbons. The silk was high quality and closely woven, in the fashionable colours of the time, which were very unlike the colours popular with quilters in 2002. There was no such thing as white silk in 1718 – it wasn't possible to bleach silk from its natural off-white colour, so all our white silk received a dip in very weak coffee, which makes a better natural white than tea. Tina and I looked through our silk collections but very little was any good. Hilary Williams of The Silk Route (see Suppliers) brought a large collection of dupions, and some of these, with plain taffeta samples from the Averil Colby fabric collection, formed the basis for the plain fabrics. We added an antique yellow satin, black velvet ribbon, cloth of gold, and much, much later some antique cloth of silver ribbon. Fabric for dyeing came from Whaley's of Bradford, including white dupion and a white twill. The remaining colours had to be dyed and the patterns reproduced as well as we could. Unfortunately, the very small quantities needed, the extreme complexity of the woven designs, the difficulty of deciphering a worn or damaged design, and the astronomical cost of hand weaving meant that we could not even consider getting true facsimiles woven. Later we got some more dupions sent from Hong Kong. Our backing was a linen sheet, dating from 1898.

The original coverlet uses recycled fabrics in two ways. There are many instances of piecing scraps together to make a large enough piece, mostly by oversewing, but some are certainly dressmaking seams. The central large tulips appear to be made from a brocade ribbon, but it was obviously not wide enough, because it was extended with another fabric.

Some fabrics had to be dyed or painted to make the replica coverlet. A push-together plastic quilt frame made an improvised silk painting frame – just the right size to fit over Pauline's bath.

SB: The replica is much brighter than the original coverlet. Was this because you had problems matching the colours?

PA: We set out to make the replica as it would have looked when new, rather than in the faded colours you see today. The original has been covered in a fine net as part of the conservation process, which also mutes the colours very slightly. While a great many pieces of silk are missing through wear and age, enough remained trapped in seam allowances to identify a matching larger piece within the coverlet, so we didn't have to make arbitrary decisions about replacement colours. These seam allowances often revealed the original colours, brighter and stronger than the faded antique silks on the surface.

A selection of the fabrics used for the replica coverlet, showing hand-dyed and commercial silks. Having ample fabrics on hand ensured that there was sufficient to complete the project.

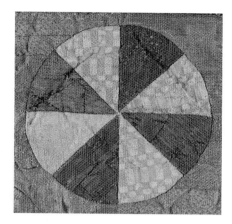

A selection of blocks from the original coverlet showing some of the fabric and colour choices of the maker. Pattern 22 (original block 45), Pattern 1 (original block 11), and Pattern 63 (original block 175). See Coverlet Layout and Numbering for explanation of the numbers used on the blocks.

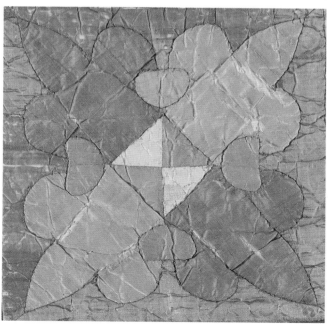

SB: Most of the fabrics are plain or shot, but how did you match the patterned silks?

PA: At first I thought it would be possible to print fabrics from photographs enlarged to full size, but the coverlet is too creased for that and many fabrics were also very badly worn or faded. The deciding factor was that each patch would have had to be enlarged enough to include the seam allowances, which would make it out of scale and look all wrong. So it was literally back to the drawing board, and in the case of stripes, back to the computer. Stripes were measured for stripe width and brocades traced from full-size photographs using a light table. I haven't counted up all the different fabrics I produced, but it probably totals over sixty. The stripes and other patterns all had to be reproduced differently.

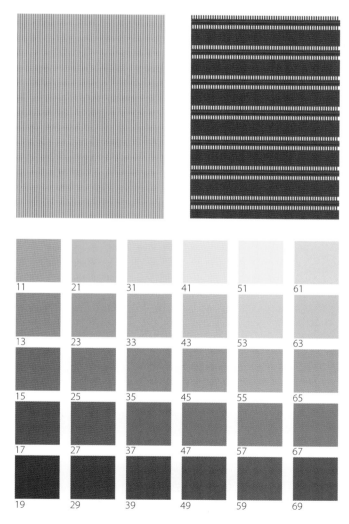

Pauline's husband drew stripes using Autocad software on the computer and he produced a set of colour swatches for her from the programme's colour palette. Tina and Pauline each had a copy and found this very useful for coordinating colours. Numbers were given to the swatches for accurate identification of colours.

I experimented with printing fabric on the computer, but learned this would be prone to fading. I also tried a transfer paper for silk, but my first attempts weren't satisfactory and the silk was left very stiff and glazed, so I tried combining dyeing, screen-printing and painting. All the silk for printing was toned down first with a dip in a coffee bath. One tan was dyed in strong tea and several other colours were obtained (with a lot of experimentation) by dye-painting with procion dyes. Some patterns were achieved with screen-printing, including printing with an opaque medium on black velvet. Markal Paintsticks were used to make coloured streaks on one red. A bronze Markal was used to stencil a brocaded pattern on a dark brown silk and a very complex brocade pattern on a wide-striped chestnut and blue silk. All this was very time consuming.

SB: The replica, like the original, is made of silk. Isn't silk more difficult to work with than cotton?

PA: We didn't realize that the original silks were much more closely woven than modern ones. The modern silks frayed! This meant that the really difficult blocks of flowers and animals were impossible to make, because the fabric frayed so badly. We used ⅜in (1cm) seam allowances to try to overcome this. Several members independently came up with the same solution – where it is impossible to tack (baste) the silk snugly to the paper, because it has to be snipped for a curve or V shape, change your stitching mode from oversewing to appliqué. It really works and hardly shows! But it is salutary to think that, while our sewing skills may be equal to those of the maker 1718, her silks, probably woven in Jacobean times, were far more interesting, varied and tightly woven than anything we could find.

Using modern-day silk fabrics proved problematic when making some of the blocks for the replica coverlet, as modern equivalents fray more than silks from the 18th century, which was a greater problem for some of the more detailed figurative blocks. Slightly wider seam allowances and adaptations in technique helped to overcome this. These two images are from the original coverlet and show some of the 'tricky' areas, such as feet, tails and beak. You can also see that some of the original fabrics have rotted away.

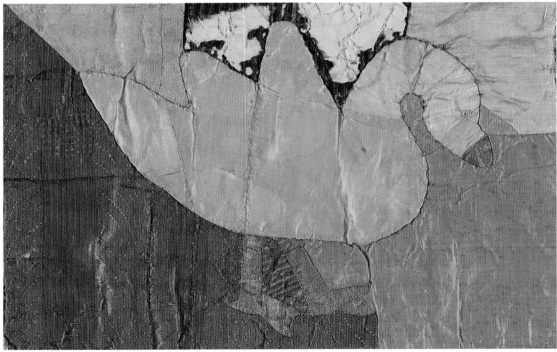

SB: Were there any problems with such a big project involving so many quilters? Group projects often take longer than expected…

PA: There have been many hiccups along the way! Some members found that they had overestimated their skills or underestimated the difficulties of the technique. I asked members to contact me to check their completed block had arrived back safely, as some kits had got lost in the post, and to send them by recorded post. There was some misinterpretation of the instructions and some remedial sewing was needed to ensure the replica was really accurate.

We had to recognize that not everyone had the same level of skill – new skills had to be learned and we needed to allow extra time in order to complete the project.

It was decided to hold two drop-in afternoon workshops for Guild members to help with the final assembly of the replica coverlet's blocks, at The Guild Conference and AGM in Torquay, Devon, England in March 2003. We supplied all the equipment and asked the quilters to just bring clean hands and a thimble. This left enough time for backing and finishing. The replica coverlet was displayed, in all its glory, at the Festival of Quilts in Birmingham, England, in 2004. The Festival has used some of the block designs for its commemorative badges too.

SB: I have been able to use all the records from the replica project as the starting point for the blocks in this book, so thank you for making sure the project was so well documented.

PA: I kept a record of all the people involved with the project, along with photo files, original block drawings, instruction sheets, colour photocopies of all the finished replica blocks, samples of the fabrics used, a sample of one of the kits, a 'handling sample' and many other items recording how we made the replica. These are now kept in the collection of The Quilters' Guild of the British Isles. We also made sure the replica was properly photographed on completion.

SB: Pauline, that was a wonderful project history especially your many tips about recreating a replica of the 1718 coverlet – so much information in fact, there will be tips, techniques and ideas you mentioned included throughout this book. I'm sure our readers will be inspired to start their own project as soon as possible.

This small sample, assembled by Pauline Adams from blocks made by members of the replica project team, shows a different construction for Block 48 (original block 97) and additional seams in the tulips on Block 42 (original block 101).

Coverlet Layout and Numbering

The 1718 Silk Patchwork Coverlet is called a coverlet rather than a quilt as it was made without wadding. The layout is generally symmetrical along a vertical axis, although there are some exceptions to this. There are five different sizes of finished blocks: 4½in (11.4cm) square, 9in (22.9cm) square, 13½in (34.3cm) square, 9in x 4½in (22.9cm x 11.4cm) rectangle and 4½in x 2¼in (11.4cm x 5.7cm) rectangle.

Block Numbering

The coverlet has many repeated blocks, so for the purposes of this book every block has been given two numbers. The one shown unbracketed on the photograph here refers to the number of that block *pattern*. The Block Directory lists the patterns in numerical order. The number in brackets refers to the individual version of the block in the replica coverlet (called the original block number, throughout the book). So every block in the quilt has a unique number. It was felt necessary to retain this numbering system for those of you wishing to recreate the coverlet, so a particular colour or fabric combination or minor design variation can be described and you will be able to locate the block in the numbered coverlet illustration. See also the Block Directory introduction for further information and also individual thumbnail pictures of all of the blocks.

Every block in the quilt is included in the Block Directory with a full-size template set. Due to the restrictions of the page size, some of the larger blocks have a quarter or half of this template shown. The goose, one of the largest figurative blocks, Pattern 66 (original blocks 176 and 180), has the template split over two pages. In all cases a scaled-down template of the full block is also included at 25%. These may be enlarged by 400% on a photocopier if you prefer.

To use all the blocks for mosaic piecing and the geometric and figurative blocks with curves for the modern techniques, you will need to trace off or photocopy the template for use. You may photocopy the templates but only for your own personal, non-commercial use.

To plan an alternative layout for the blocks, use a square grid, in which each unit represents a 4½in (11.4cm) square. Larger blocks, such as Pattern 1 (original blocks 1 and 11), Pattern 48 (original blocks 97, 103 and 161) or Pattern 66 (original blocks 176 and 180) will cover multiple squares. Refer to the Techniques section for all the practical help you will need.

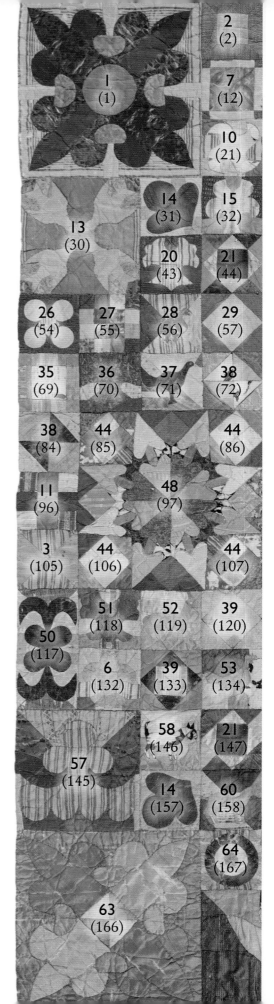

No.	(Ref)	No.	(Ref)	No.	(Ref)	No.	(Ref)	No.	(Ref)	No.	(Ref)	No.	(Ref)	No.	(Ref)	No.	(Ref)	No.	(Ref)	No.	(Ref)
3	(3)	4	(4)	5	(5)	6	(6)	5	(7)	4	(8)	3	(9)	2	(10)	1	(11)				
8	(13)	3	(14)	7	(15)	9	(16)	7	(17)	3	(18)	8	(19)	7	(20)						
11	(22)	8	(23)	12	(24)	11	(25)	12	(26)	8	(27)	11	(28)	10	(29)						
16	(33)	17	(34)	18	(35)	19	(36)	18	(37)	17	(38)	16	(39)	15	(40)	14	(41)	13	(42)		
22	(45)	23	(46)	24	(47)	25	(48)	24	(49)	23	(50)	22	(51)	21	(52)	20	(53)				
30	(58)	31	(59)	32	(60)	33	(61)	34	(62)	31	(63)	30	(64)	29	(65)	28	(66)	27	(67)	26	(68)
39	(73)	40	(74)	41	(75)	42	(76)	43	(77)	40	(78)	39	(79)	38	(80)	37	(81)	36	(82)	35	(83)
39	(87)	45	(88)	46	(89)	46	(90)	47	(91)	39	(92)	44	(93)	44	(94)	38	(95)				
30	(98)	42	(99)	49	(100)	42	(101)	30	(102)	48	(103)	11	(104)								
39	(108)	47	(109)	46	(110)	46	(111)	45	(112)	39	(113)	44	(114)	44	(115)	3	(116)				
29	(121)	40	(122)	43	(123)	42	(124)	41	(125)	40	(126)	29	(127)	39	(128)	52	(129)	51	(130)	50	(131)
30	(135)	3	(136)	54	(137)	55	(138)	56	(139)	3	(140)	30	(141)	53	(142)	39	(143)	6	(144)		
59	(148)	38	(149)	44	(150)	44	(151)	38	(152)	59	(153)	21	(154)	58	(155)	57	(156)				
61	(159)	62	(160)	48	(161)	62	(162)	61	(163)	60	(164)	14	(165)								
65	(168)	24	(169)	44	(170)	44	(171)	24	(172)	65	(173)	64	(174)	63	(175)						
66	(176)	67	(177)	68	(178)	67	(179)	66	(180)												
69	(181)	69	(182)																		

Fabrics and Materials

The original fabrics used for the coverlet are almost all silk and were all clothing materials. Whether you use the closest modern equivalents for your patchwork or select from the wonderful array of quilting cottons now available for a contemporary interpretation, we have a choice of fabric beyond the dreams of the original maker.

Fabrics for your Project

Before selecting the fabrics for your 1718 project, consider the technique you want to use and the planned purpose of the item you are going to make. If you decide to make a replica, you would need silk fabrics, linen thread, acid-free paper and a linen sheet for backing. The finished coverlet could not be washed or dry-cleaned, because of the papers left inside, so everyday household use is really ruled out. Silk would have to be dyed and printed for an exact replica, although if the challenge is seen to be in the stitching then exact colour matching would not be an issue. Patchwork cotton is the best choice for modern everyday use. Whichever approach you use, you will need to be creative in selecting your fabrics.

You will also need to make decisions about colour. If you love the original's softly muted colours, faded over time, you could use these as the starting point for your colour scheme. Remember that some fabrics, including many of the black silks, have rotted away almost completely, revealing the paper in some places and the linen backing in others. If you are seeking this worn, antique effect, you could try linen for some of the piecing, or incorporate fabrics with 18th century-style text, imitating the papers. The replica's colours show how the coverlet would probably have looked when new and is a good reference if you prefer brighter colours (see Making the Replica Coverlet). Alternatively, use your own unique colour scheme.

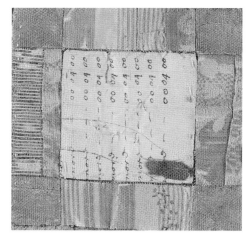

In this block, the centre square, originally pink, has worn away to show the paper in Pattern 35 (original block 69) and two blue and white striped rectangles are made from seamed scraps. Look for fabrics with printed text for a similar but contemporary effect.

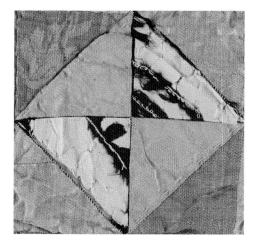

Some fragments of black silk show remnants of thread where scraps were seamed together with backstitch, such as Pattern 38 (original block 80).

Here, the black centre square has rotted to reveal the linen backing sheet in Pattern 31 (original block 63). Note the seams in the two striped yellow and white squares. There are many blocks where smaller scraps were seamed together before piecing.

Silk

Silks are not washable, although they would make a beautiful wall hanging or special occasion item, and the sheen of silk certainly makes the patchwork colours glow. The main problem is fraying. Modern silks tend to fray easily, so if you intend to machine piece your patchwork, a larger ⅜in (1cm) seam allowance than the ¼in (6mm) used for the block cutting lists is better – this can be added on when cutting out using templates (see Techniques: Rotary Cutting with Templates). Silk dupion and more coarsely woven silks fray too much for appliqué, so more tightly woven silks are preferable, such as some Thai and Japanese silks. Look for crisp, tightly woven silks for smaller patchwork pieces and appliqué. Consider lightweight furnishing silks, too. The mosaic patchwork papers stabilize the silk for sewing and finer silks can be stabilized for machine piecing with a layer of iron-on stabilizer on the back (such as Vilene). As pure silk is not produced specifically for patchwork, there are fewer colours available and you may need to dye your own silk (see Dyeing and Printing). Some silk and cotton blends are made for patchwork and may handle more easily than pure silk.

A selection of modern silks.

Cotton

Patchwork cottons and other lightweight cotton fabrics will provide a washable alternative. Fine and tightly woven cottons are easier to use than looser weaves. They are generally more lightfast than silks so will be less prone to fading, and patchwork cottons are available in a wide range of solid colours as well as prints and fancy weaves. Silver metallic prints could be used to imitate the woven silver threads in the original. Lawn is more finely woven than patchwork cotton and is especially good for fine appliqué, but is not available in such a large range of colours. Plain cottons may benefit from 'distressing' by being dyed in a very weak, very pale beige dye, to tone down more vibrant colours. A weak coffee solution was used to tone down some silks for the replica project and this gives a less pinkish tone than dipping in tea.

Shot or two-tone cottons make a good substitute for the shot silks used extensively for the original coverlet. There are several ranges of shot cottons produced for patchwork (see Suppliers). Warp and weft threads of similar colour and tone have subtle shading while stronger contrasts are more dramatic. Woven stripes feature in many blocks. While some stripes are woven specially for patchwork, you may find more choice if you explore printed stripes and shirting

A selection of patchwork cottons.

fabrics, perhaps even recycling shirts. If you decide to use recycled clothing fabrics, check their fibre content labels and avoid high percentages of polyester or other synthetic fibres, which may make the fabric more difficult to sew. Recycling fabric would be in the spirit of the original coverlet.

You may prefer to interpret the blocks in more modern colours and prints, although very bold printed designs would need to be chosen with care. Small tone-on-tone prints and batiks could be used to imitate the mottled beauty of the faded and worn fabrics for a shabby-chic look, although there are almost no printed fabrics in the original coverlet.

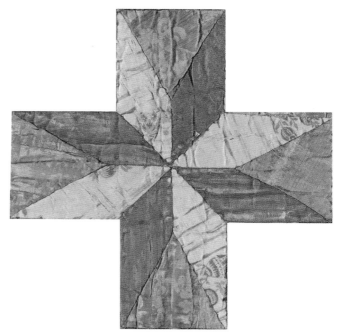

The most unusual fabric in the coverlet is the printed or painted silk used for four sections in the central star Pattern 49 (original block 100), as well as small pieces used elsewhere in the coverlet. The stylized design of flowers and foliage in red and green includes a poppy-like seed head, set between widely spaced red and yellow satin stripes on an ivory background. The red seems to have been applied over the green because there are glimpses of red next to the green. This was surely one of the maker's favourite materials, as it has pride of place in the centre of the coverlet.

Subtle blue-and-white stripes create a frame effect behind the quatrefoil fleur-de-lys in Pattern 1 (original block 11). Each fleur-de-lys features a wide brown satin stripe, with the grain aligned into the point.

Dyeing and Printing

If you enjoy dyeing and printing your own fabrics, you could try these techniques to make replica materials. Procion dyes work with silk and cotton and may be used to over-dye or tone down the colour and pattern of commercial patchwork fabrics, as well as dyeing white cloth. You would need to experiment to get the correct colours. Digital printing on your home computer printer could be used to create similar patterns to some of the weaves or the fabric in the star point in Pattern 49 (original block 100), either printing onto specially prepared fabric sheets or preparing your own with a suitable solution (see Suppliers). A similar pattern to the yellow fabric in Pattern 7 (original blocks 12 and 20) and Pattern 8 (original block 13) may be more easily achieved by block printing. Screen-printing could also be used to create patterns inspired by the original fabrics.

Patterns that reference the yellow woven silk motif featured in Pattern 7 (original blocks 12 and 20) could be created by block printing or screen-printing. Some batik ranges have similar prints.

The original fabrics

All of the fabrics in the coverlet are silk, except for one wool-pile velvet, two colourways of a fabric with a worsted wool weft with silk warp and wefts and one simple striped fabric with a silk warp and a linen weft. Originally made for clothing, some may have been lining fabrics. The pattern is all in the weaving, with damasks, satins and other fancy weaves, with only one very unusual printed or painted dress fabric used in the central star block. In the early 18th century, fashions in fabrics changed more than the cut of the clothes and there was a strong tradition of reusing and recycling fabric. As there are few relevant costumes of the period surviving in museum textile and costume collections, and these tend to be the most high-status fabrics, the coverlet's fabrics are unusual survivors, even though many are now in poor condition.

This velvet with a linen warp and a wool pile used in the centre of Pattern 21 (original block 44) has a bold crimson arabesque pattern. Try block printing or stamping onto cotton velveteen for a similar effect.

The silk used for the upper background of Pattern 57 (original block 145) (top picture) now has mid-blue vertical stripes and simplified flowers on a soft pinkish ground, with what look like irregularly placed tiny black dots. This would have been a rich red and the black dots are all that remain of a silver thread that has tarnished and broken away. The original cloth would have gleamed with silver against the red. Its 'twin' (original block 156) seems to share the same yellow stripe for the swag but has not survived so well.

The original colours

The subdued colours of the coverlet look very different today from how they were in 1718, when they would have been much brighter, although they still harmonize beautifully. The replica (see Making the Replica) aimed to recapture the vivid appearance of the original. Most colours have faded, especially some reds, yellows, salmon pinks and richer reds, changing the value contrasts in some blocks, but the deterioration of some fabrics also revealed brighter fragments in seam allowances, enabling us to catch glimpses of their original vibrancy. Depending on your patchwork style, the faded colours may be more appealing than the original high contrasts.

The original fabric patterns

The fabrics were all handwoven and pre-date later 18th-century industrial innovations in spinning and weaving, such as the spinning jenny and the jacquard loom. Hand loom weavers could control the patterns by shafts or foot pedals for simple damask and satin weaves. A study of the coverlet's fabrics revealed that there are over ninety shaft-woven fabrics and thirty plain ('tabby') weave fabrics – a wide variety, from the plainest taffetas to shot silks with different coloured warp and wefts. There are many stripes, including shot stripes and ribbed silks, and patterns created with warps of different fibres and thicknesses. Flat metal strips or 'tinsel' (probably silver), are used as a weft stripe in several pieces. Other woven patterns include tiny spots, sometimes organized in diagonal stripes or chevrons, and a design called 'Ms and Os', which contrasts areas of plain weaving with patterns made of short weft floats.

The central square in Pattern 30 (original block 98) was an imitation gold cloth with tinsel strips (technically called 'floats'), with the main weave continuing underneath. This was a common patterning technique found on the coverlet. It was replaced by gold lamé in the replica.

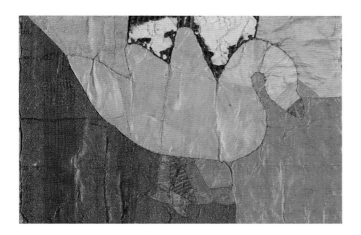

There are two similar blue and brown woven stripes, one with a diamond pattern in the blue as seen in Pattern 57 (original block 145) and one with a ripple effect in the blue stripe as used in Pattern 66 (original block 176) shown here. Perhaps the juxtaposition of this stripe and the green silk makes the goose look like it is stepping out of water.

The original colours and dyes

Textile historian Deryn O'Connor researched considerable information about dyeing from a reprint of an early 18th century book on dye techniques, which compiled information from earlier German and French books and included information on dyeing in England. The coverlet has many colours and most of these seem to have been yarn-dyed before weaving rather than dyeing the finished cloth, a technique that lends itself to the making of shot silks. If you are interested in natural dyes and wish to try dyeing some fabrics for your patchwork, there is plenty of information available for the modern dyer. While it would not be possible to achieve the shot effects by dyeing plain silk naturally from scratch, similar effects could be achieved by over-dyeing paler-coloured shot silks with primary colours.

Yellow – there are a large number of yellows in the coverlet, ranging from soft lemon to strong egg yolk yellow, both on their own and combined with white, pale blue, black and a bright blueish-crimson red. Yellow dyes included dyer's weld (*Reseda luteola*), wild marigolds and turmeric.

Yellow and red was a very fashionable colour combination at the time the coverlet was made and there are several stripes combining these colours, such as the striped fabrics in the tulip Pattern 40 (original block 126). This could be copied using fabric paints or markers.

Blue – this is the next most common colour, varying from a very light blue, through medium and on to deep blue, although there are only two pieces of deep blue in the coverlet. Blues were obtained either from locally grown woad (*Isatis tinctoria*) or indigo (*Indigofera tinctoria*), imported from the east. Woad is more difficult than indigo to dye deep blue, so the lighter blues may be woad, but these colours are also easy to dye with indigo. Repeated dippings in the dye bath are used to build up colour for both dyes. One blue stripe features a shaded blue thread. Two different dark blue and brown stripes are used extensively in the coverlet, suggesting that the maker had a large amount of this fabric.

Green – there are many greens used, from blueish-green to yellow green, but only one very dark green. In the 18th century there was no dye for green, which was always a mixture of yellow and blue dyed one over the other. This was because the two dyestuffs were from different dye families and could not be combined in one dye bath. The light greens have retained an attractive freshness.

Red – only two of the three reds have kept their colour, including a strong brick red at the top of Pattern 57 (original block 156), which would have been dyed with madder (*Rubia tinctorum*). Reds were made with three main dyes – madder root for warmer reds, brazilwood or 'brasilwood' (*Caesalpinia brasiliensis*) used for a range of reds and cochineal for crimson. Confusingly, sappan wood was also imported and referred to as brazil. It would be impossible to distinguish between the two in the 1718 fabrics without using chemical analysis. The faded red was probably dyed with brazilwood, which produced a crimson with an ash mordant. It was colourfast but not lightfast and faded quickly. For this reason, it was forbidden in France – English dyers seem to have been less scrupulous! Polish cochineal was replaced in the 17th century with the cochineal beetle (*Dactylopius coccus*) imported from America, almost certainly used for the strong crimsons. The red used for the tulips in Pattern 40 (original blocks 74 and 126) may be cochineal dyed.

Pink and purple – the salmon pink and the light purple have almost disappeared. The light purple was probably also dyed with brazilwood. The pinks, now faded to ivory, are likely to have been dyed with safflower (*Carthamus tinctorius*), a dye particularly common during the 17th century and also forbidden in France due to its poor qualities. It was another imported dyestuff but was also grown in Oxfordshire, England from the 1660s to the early 1700s.

Brown – the browns have survived rather well. Walnut (bark, roots, leaves and nuts) is recommended in the French dye manual for making browns, and greys could be made with madder root finished with walnut.

Black – many of the black pieces have rotted away due to the iron used to fix the dye, with only fragments remaining next to the stitching to indicate where it was used. It was dyed in a complex recipe by combining galls, sumach, madder, antimony, gum tragacanth, alder bark, vitriol and filings of iron. The galls were a strong source of tannic acid, which eventually reacted with the iron filings to rot the fabric. The replica coverlet gives a better impression of how the bold blacks and dark browns would have originally looked (see Making the Replica Coverlet).

The black silk has rotted on the cat's body in Pattern 58 (original block 146) and the rabbit Pattern 61 (original block 163), making these blocks look very different from when they were newly made.

Only four solid black patches have survived in a recognizable form including Pattern 30 (original block 141), which gives them a rather startling quality in the patchwork.

Other Materials

If making a replica coverlet or blocks from the design, you will need a few basic items, as follows.

Sewing thread – we have a far greater choice of threads for patchwork than was available in the early 18th century. For machine-pieced versions of the coverlet in cotton fabric, a good quality machine sewing cotton thread, 50 or 60 count, will be ideal. The original thread is now off-white in colour, but you may prefer to use a mid-grey or sage green for piecing if you want your stitches to be less obvious. If you decide to use silk, silk thread may be used for machine piecing, but it has a tendency to slip in the stitching.

For hand piecing using the original mosaic patchwork method, you have a wider choice of threads. Linen thread, as used for the coverlet, is difficult to find so two-ply lacemaking thread was substituted for the replica project, but this proved difficult to use for hand stitching. If the original maker had any other choice then she would have used silk thread for the stitching, which is the best alternative option. If you are using cotton fabric for mosaic piecing, a cotton thread (as above) is appropriate. It may be waxed with beeswax or a silicone wax block to make it less likely to snag and knot. Finer hand quilting threads may also be used for whip stitching the mosaic piecing together.

Paper – if you want to use the original technique of mosaic piecing for your patchwork throughout your project, you will need to cut your templates in paper. For a washable patchwork, use regular paper for the papers and standard tacking (basting) through all three layers, removing the papers after the blocks have been stitched together. Alternatively, if you want to make a historical recreation of the original, where the papers were left in place, you will need to use an acid-free paper that is firm enough for easy handling when tacking (basting) the seam allowances and whip stitching the patchwork. Explore different artists' papers until you find the right one for you. Very soft paper may be easy to tack through, but it will be difficult to use for the more intricate pieced blocks.

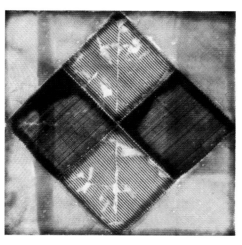

©Textile Conservation Foundation
Photography by Michael Halliwell

This transmitted light image shows the papers in Pattern 29 (original block 121), revealing the fold lines in the paper templates. The papers were intended to be left in the patchwork.

Backing and wadding (batting) – the 1718 coverlet is now backed with numerous pieces of linen stitched together, but at some point in its history it has had an additional backing, revealed by the green silk thread remnants on the back. You could use a linen sheet to back the patchwork for a similar effect, as was used for the replica. If you wish to add wadding (batting) and quilt the coverlet, something thin but supportive, such as prewashed flannel, would be appropriate. This would give a soft resting place for the silk and give a little more 'body' to the coverlet, while providing better support for the mosaic piecing than a thin non-woven wadding. Unlike seamed patchwork or machine piecing, mosaic patchwork has no fabric directly under the whipped seams, so it may need a firmer support in use. If your patchwork is machine pieced and hand or machine appliquéd instead, it may be layered and quilted in the usual way, but a thin wadding may be better than one with more loft, since the original unquilted coverlet naturally appears fairly flat (see Techniques: Simple Quilting Ideas).

A selection of hand sewing and machine sewing threads.

Techniques

This section describes all the techniques you will need to make either your own modern version of the 1718 coverlet or a replica of it. The 1718 coverlet was made using the technique we now know as mosaic patchwork (sometimes called English paper piecing), with each block made from fabric tacked (basted) over papers and then oversewn or whip stitched together by hand. While mosaic patchwork has experienced a revival recently, with many patchworkers rediscovering the portable technique by sewing 'hexies' (hexagons), the blocks can also be made using modern machine patchwork and hand or machine appliqué techniques. You can use whichever method you prefer, although the modern techniques will be more suited to wadding (batting) and quilting. The blocks in the Block Directory describe both methods. Refer also to The Layout of the Coverlet, which explains the numbering system used for the blocks. The Techniques section and Block Directory can also be used as inspiration to create your own smaller projects using the blocks from the 1718 coverlet. You could make a whole range of smaller lap quilts, cushions, bags, or whatever you like (see the banner project shown here).

Mosaic Patchwork

The method referred to as the 'original method' throughout the Block Directory has the tacking (basting) stitches going through the seam allowance and the backing paper only, with the papers left inside the patchwork. If you intend to give the patchwork modern use, you will want to remove the papers before finishing, so if you are using cotton fabric, tacking through all the layers is fine. For silk, it is still best not to tack through the front of the patch, as this may mark the fabric – make a test piece first.

Equipment

- Normal hand sewing kit, 'sharps' hand sewing needles (No.9 or 10 are useful sizes), tacking (basting) and sewing thread.

- Fabric scissors, sharp paper scissors and a pencil to label the papers.

- A tray or mat to lay out the fabrics, on top of a scrap of wadding (batting) or felt to stop slipping.

- If using silk, paperclips or miniature clothes pegs (clothespins) are better for holding pieces together than pins.

- A pressing cloth will also be needed for silk fabrics.

This banner project, called Cantata and made by Maureen Poole, uses ideas from the 1718 coverlet to create a modern interpretation.

Papers and tacking (basting)

1 Make a copy of the block template and mark the top edge. You will sew from the back, so make sure that your template is a mirror image of the finished block, so that balance marks and other notes can be seen from the back of the block while you sew. Note that many blocks are mirrored pairs. You will need to add balance marks, direction arrows (for striped fabrics) and perhaps identify each piece with a label or numbering system that makes sense to you (see example below). The balance marks need to be matched up across the seam lines when the block is assembled and are especially important on curved seams and complex blocks.

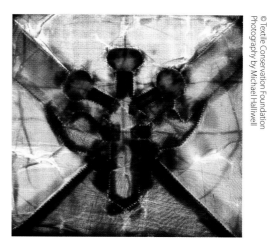

A transmitted light image of the papers in Pattern 43 (original block 77), showing the lining-up marks on the templates – horizontal and vertical lines and a roughly sketched circle.

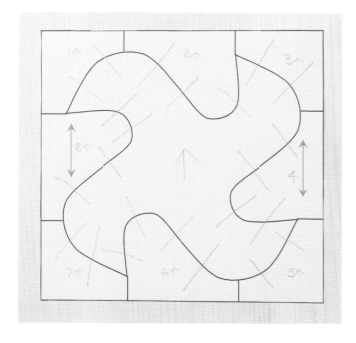

2 Cut out the papers. Trim off any spare paper around the block template and then cut out the first piece, which will be at one edge. If there are isolated paper pieces to cut out (such as circles), make a short scalpel cut along the line and then use thin-bladed scissors to complete the cut. The thickness of the fabric can add extra bulk to the edges of each piece, so the pieces don't fit well when sewn. If this is a problem, cutting the papers *exactly* either side of the printed line, so about $^1\!/_{32}$in (1mm) is lost, will fix the fit.

A transmitted light image of the papers in Pattern 44 (original block 107), showing the construction symbols on the templates.

3 Use the templates to cut out the fabric pieces one at a time, adding a $^3\!/_8$in (1cm) seam allowance all round. Make sure stripes go in the right direction. Hold the paper firmly against the fabric as you cut, to avoid the need to pin. Alternatively, use paperclips after the first edge is cut. If you are using cotton and will be removing the papers at the end, waxy freezer paper can be used, ironed onto the back of each fabric piece before cutting out and peeled away later. It will not be possible to tack (baste) just through the seam and paper with this method. Alternatively, use a small piece of double-sided sticky tape to stick the template to the fabric temporarily.

4 Tack (baste) each piece to its paper before cutting out another paper, so you don't lose pieces. Use tacking thread and a running stitch. The stitches must only go through the seam allowance and the paper, with none showing on the front. Tack round all edges. Your aim is to get a snug fit of fabric against paper. Start tacking along a straight edge, if there is one – press the seam allowance over the edge of the paper, using a pressing cloth if required or finger press. The coverlet maker didn't have the luxury of an electric iron, so she would probably have been finger pressing or using a wooden pressing 'iron' at this stage.

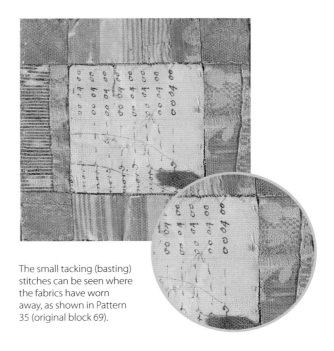

The small tacking (basting) stitches can be seen where the fabrics have worn away, as shown in Pattern 35 (original block 69).

5 Where the shapes are curved, snip the seam allowance at intervals, so that the tacked (basted) curves can follow the exact paper shapes, or run a gathering thread round the curve. Snip into inside corners. It helps to put off clipping until just before you sew the curve, take a small tacking backstitch where needed to hold down any of the little clipped flaps, and clip no nearer to the edge of the paper than ⅛in (3mm). Your aim is to get a snug fit of fabric against paper, and still have some sound fabric to stitch into.

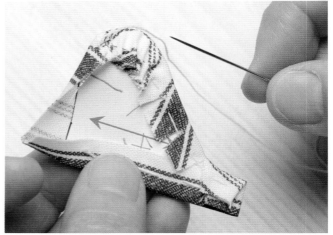

6 If your block has very narrow pieces (such as occur with the stems of flowers or the legs and ears of an animal), press the seam allowance to the first side, tack (baste) it, trim off excess seam allowance and turn and tack the remaining sides to the first seam allowance only.

Oversewing the patchwork

- Stitch pieces right sides together using a small oversewing stitch through the folded edges of the fabric only, making 15–20 stitches to 1in (2.5cm). Practise on a simple block first.

- An order for sewing is suggested in the individual pattern instructions in the Block Directory.

- Overcast or whip stitch the pieces, starting and finishing the sewing with a knot. Begin about ¼in (6mm) from the corner of the patch and stitch back towards the start of the seam before proceeding.

- Don't use very long threads, as oversewing puts a lot of wear on your thread – about 18in (45cm) is fine.

- Use paperclips or mini clothes pegs (clothespins) to keep pieces in position. Be sure to match up balance marks as you sew, especially for more complex blocks, or pieces will be out of alignment and blocks won't lie flat when finished. Sewing from each end towards the centre of the seam, overlapping stitches in the middle, also helps align pieces properly.

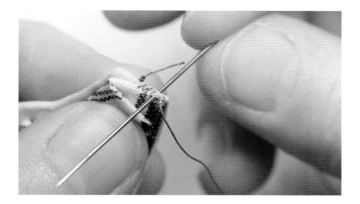

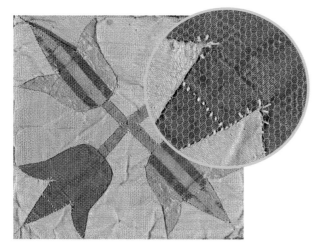

At inside corners you will need to make extra and longer stitches into the V to prevent fraying, as shown on the red tulip in Pattern 40 (original block 74).

Sewing curves and figurative motifs

Many blocks have curves in them. It helps to start at an end or a balance mark and to sew only a few stitches before adjusting the two pieces to realign the curve. The most striking and unusual blocks are flowers, animals, birds or figures, within a patchwork format of triangles or wedges. In most cases, sewing the flower or figure together first is not the easiest way to make the block. Sewing stems, leaves, limbs and so on, to the adjacent background section is usually the best way to start as it helps position these correctly within the block (see individual instructions in the Block Directory). Balance marks and seam junctions between motif and background must be matched carefully.

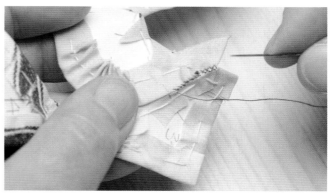

Embroidering eyes

The animals and birds, but not the human figures, have eyes embroidered with tiny buttonhole wheels (see diagram). Use a single strand of fine embroidery silk or cotton. The embroidered eyes could be replaced with tiny beads.

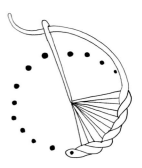

Adapting Mosaic Patchwork

The replica project stitchers found that modern silks, more loosely woven than the originals, frayed so much that in some places, like the inside of curves and into corners, there was nothing to tack (baste) into but a fringe of threads between clippings. Tacking (basting) therefore had to be modified for deep curves and dispensed with when there was insufficient seam allowance left after clipping into a V. Stitching was changed from traditional oversewing on the wrong side, to appliquéing on the right side in those places, where the tacking has been modified for a curve or is not possible in a V or a corner. The following tips are adapted from the replica project notes.

- When stitching, if you come to a curve where the fabric isn't turned snug to the paper, turn the work over and carefully appliqué the outside curved piece onto sound fabric, following the curve of the inside curved shape's paper. Fig 1 shows the back of an inside curve tacked, with X marking the spots when appliqué should start and stop.

- Very tight curves on narrow pieces (such as those that enclose the ends of animals' legs) should be treated as a notch (see Fig 1).

- Narrow notches and Vs are the most challenging, as a point has to be inserted into a V notch. Fig 2 shows the wrong side of a V notch tacked (basted). Clip down the centre of the V but stop where the seam allowance becomes less than ⅛in (3mm) on each side of the snip. Tack down towards the bottom of the V, but when the turning is too small to tack, change your stitching method (shown by X points on Fig 2), carry the thread across to the other side and start tacking back out. Don't cut the tacking thread, but pull it naturally tight to the width of the V.

- When stitching the pointed piece into the V, work normal oversewing down the V, until you get to where the seam allowances cease to be snug to the paper edge of the V. Turn the work over so you are working from the front. Pull the loose point up and over the seam allowance on either side of the V and the tacking thread lying across the V. Bring your needle and thread to the right side. Very neatly appliqué the pointed piece into the V shape and out again. On holding the work up to the light you will be able to see that the point fits right over the V.

- On many points you will need to needle-turn excess seam allowance at the point to the inside. It may help to trim a little of this excess, so the seam/turning allowance is towards a ⅛in (3mm) appliqué turning allowance, but beware of trimming too much.

Fig 1

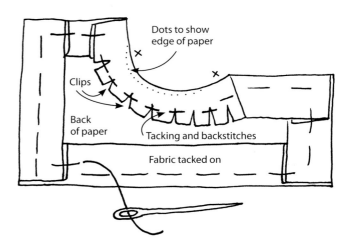

Fig 2

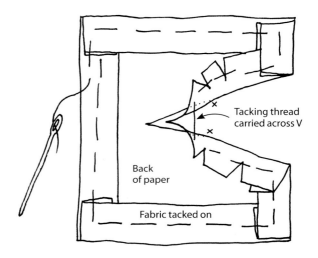

Pattern 45 from the replica coverlet includes several sharp points in the design and requires extra care in making.

Modern Techniques

The blocks can be made just as beautifully using modern rotary-cut and machine-sewn patchwork, plus various appliqué techniques, both by hand and machine. Indeed, to our modern eyes, the figurative blocks and the fleur-de-lys designs would seem more suited to appliqué than patchwork. Some blocks, like the geometric ones, are easily made with patchwork only, others with appliqué, while some combine both techniques. These methods can be used for cotton or silk fabrics, although for silk patchwork by machine you may want to use a ⅜in (1cm) seam allowance instead of ¼in (6mm) given in the pattern instructions, as the silk will fray more – use the templates to cut silk and add the seam allowance as you cut. Silk can also be backed with the lightest weight iron-on stabilizer, which helps reduce fraying. Choose a mid-grey thread for patchwork and match appliqué thread colours to the appliqué shapes.

Equipment

- Basic sewing kit.

- Sewing machine with a quarter-inch foot attachment.

- Rotary cutter, ruler and cutting mat.

- Fine pins (such as silk pins, which are fine enough not to leave holes in your fabrics).

- An iron for pressing blocks.

- Fabric markers or pencils that will show on your chosen fabrics and can be easily removed.

- Freezer paper or fusible web (depending on the appliqué technique you use).

Rotary cutting straight pieces

Cutting lists for rotary cutting are given in each set of pattern instructions. For blocks including triangles, it is often best to make the blocks in pairs, as cutting squares diagonally to make triangles will give two identical pieces.

Cutting safety

A rotary cutter has a *very* sharp blade and it is easy to accidentally cut yourself or others, so please follow these safety guidelines.

- Hold the cutter firmly in the same hand you write with, at a 45-degree angle, and hold the acrylic quilter's ruler in place with your other hand.

- Cut with the blade against the side of your ruler – on the right if you are right-handed and on the left if you are left-handed. The patchwork piece you are cutting is under the rule.

- Use a sharp blade that is free from nicks and other damage – a dull blade requires more pressure when you cut and risks the blade slipping.

- Stand up to cut if you can and place the mat on a firm surface – a kitchen counter or sturdy table is ideal.

- Always cut *away* from yourself.

- Always replace the safety guard on the cutter, and make a habit of doing this after every cut.

- Wear something on your feet when you cut, in case you drop the cutter.

- Keep cutting equipment away from children and pets.

Pattern 27 (original block 55) is one of the simplest blocks to rotary cut.

Rotary cutting with templates

- Straight-sided shapes can be cut using templates and a quilter's ruler for perfectly straight edges, adding on a ¼in (6mm) seam allowance as you go (see picture below).

- If working with silk, rotary cut all pieces this way, adding on ⅜in (1cm) all round, to allow for fraying.

- Pin the template to the fabric with flat-headed or small-headed pins, line the ruler up with the template edge and cut. Alternatively, stick the template to the fabric temporarily with a small piece of double-sided tape.

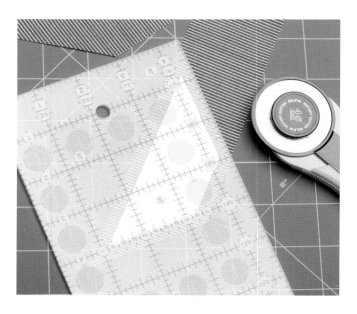

Machine-pieced patchwork

- Lay out the pieces before you begin sewing, following the block illustration, and join them together following the individual pattern instructions, to avoid sewing pieces together in the wrong order.

- Assemble each block following the individual pattern instructions. Use ¼in (6mm) seam throughout, unless you are using silk and have opted to cut pieces with a larger ⅜in (1cm) seam allowance.

- Place the first two pieces right sides together, making sure the edges to be sewn line up. Align the fabric edges with the edge of the quarter-inch foot and sew the seam.

- Use a fabric scrap as a 'leader', so the first patchwork stitches do not get chewed up.

- Pin longer seams at right angles to the stitching line and remove pins as you sew. Take care not to stretch any bias edges, such as on triangles.

- Sew curves, such as Pattern 22 (original blocks 45 and 51), with the concave piece on top of the convex piece (the corners on top of the circle segments).

- Speed up your piecing by chain piecing when you can (see picture), sewing the next pair of pieces a stitch or two after the last pair, making a 'chain' to be cut up afterwards.

- Press seams to one side, in alternate directions, so the pieces sit neatly together in the block when you come to join them together.

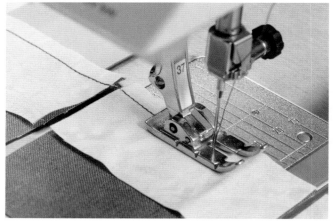

Machine piecing mitres

There are several block patterns that have mitred outer strips, or need to be sewn with inset seams. These pieces will be cut using templates, so mark the seam allowances with dots in the inner corner points.

I Pin the first strip to the centre square, lining up the corner marks with the ¼in (6mm) allowance at the ends. Sew the first two pieces together between these marks, starting and finishing with a few backstitches.

2 Insert the adjacent piece the same way, marking and sewing between the dots.

3 Sew the mitred seam by folding the central square diagonally and lining up the two sides of the mitre. You may find it easier to sew from the outer edge towards the inner corner points. A few backstitches will be required at that corner.

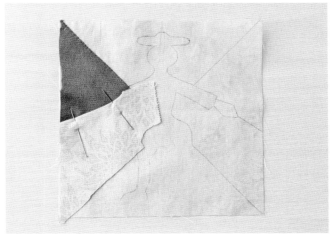

Appliqué

You can choose whichever appliqué technique suits you to make the blocks. Instructions are given here for Appliqué onto foundation squares, Needle-turn appliqué, Freezer paper appliqué and Bonded appliqué.

Appliqué onto foundation squares

Many of the figurative blocks have pieced backgrounds made from shapes that are difficult to piece. These are easier to make in appliqué.

- Use one of the background fabrics as your foundation square, as suggested in the individual block instructions. Cut the other background pieces with ¼in (6mm) seam allowances.

- Appliqué each piece to the background in turn, folding under a ¼in (6mm) hem where each piece overlaps the previous one, starting with the first piece overlapping the background. Don't fold under the seam allowances at the block edges, as these need to be sewn to the next block. Any edges that will be overlapped by the central animal or bird will be left raw, too.

- If you enjoy machine-sewn foundation piecing onto paper, you could adapt the block backgrounds for that technique.

- Alternatively, replace 4½in (11.4cm) block backgrounds with blocks made from Pattern 3 (four triangles).

Needle-turn appliqué

The needle-turn appliqué method gives a firm, strong and neat edge to an appliquéd shape.

1 You will need to add a ⅛in (3mm) turning allowance all around each piece, except for raw edges that are tucked under other appliqué pieces. As curved appliqué shapes have mostly bias edges and the turn-under is small, it is not necessary to clip the fabric around curves – just ease it under. Only deep V shapes need clipping. Tack (baste) the shape to the background with small stitches about ¼in (6mm) long and exactly ¼in (6mm) from the cut edge. The tacking stitches will prevent too much fabric from being turned under.

2 Use an appliqué needle or a long sharp to turn under the raw edge a little at a time as you sew. Use the point of the needle to stroke the fabric edge into place. Crease the turned edge with your fingers as you go. Start and finish sewing on a long edge, with a few knots and a few tiny running stitches hidden under the edge of the appliqué. Come up through the folded edge of the appliqué shape and stitch down into the backing fabric, keeping the stitches at right angles to the folded edge so they are almost invisible.

3 Create sharp points and corners by leaving the last couple of stitches loose, pushing the point of the fabric under the shape as far as possible and then gently tightening up the sewing thread. The loose stitches will tighten up and the point will pull out perfectly. For a deep V, turn the edges under as neatly as possible and add some extra and slightly longer stitches inside the V.

Appliqué stems

Narrow stems, such as the flower stems on Pattern 40 (original block 74) and Pattern 42 (original block 76), are easy to make.

1 Cut a strip as directed in the block instructions. Fold the strip in half lengthwise and then press.

2 Draw a line on the background fabric along the centre of the finished stem strip. Pin the folded strip to the background fabric, lining up the raw edge with the centre line you have just drawn. Machine sew the strip to the background, lining up the stitches a third of the way across the width of the strip, closer to the raw edge than the fold.

3 Flip the strip over, press, and hand sew the folded edge to the backing fabric. These stems could also be made with ready-made fusible bias tape, but take care to keep them straight.

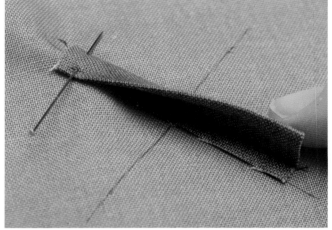

Freezer paper appliqué

This method uses freezer paper templates behind the fabric, which is folded and pressed over the paper edge for accuracy. It is not suitable for very tiny shapes, as it is almost impossible to remove the paper. The waxy wrappers from copier paper can be substituted for freezer paper.

- Freezer paper has a waxy side that can be ironed to the back of the fabric, sticking the template in place.

- Cut these templates as mirror images of the block templates and without adding any extra to the edges.

- Cut out the fabric after ironing on the template, adding a ¼in (6mm) turning allowance all around.

- Sew the appliqué shape in place by hand, or by machine with a small appliqué stitch or tiny zigzag.

- Cut away the background fabric behind the appliqué, leaving about a ¼in (6mm) overlap, and gently pull the paper out. Alternatively, cut a slit in the background fabric and remove the paper through that.

- Fold and press the fabric over the edge of the freezer paper. Finger pressing may suffice, or use the tip of an iron.

Adding definition to appliqué

Defining the edge of a motif with a machine-sewn straight-stitch line (as below) gives a firm edge to the appliqué shape and would help stop silk appliqué fraying so easily. Iron on a freezer paper template (as above) and machine sew very close to the line with a matching thread. Cut out the piece with a small turning allowance, between ¼in (6mm) and ⅛in (3mm) depending on how easily it frays. Peel away the freezer paper. Now follow the steps for needle-turn appliqué, tacking (basting) the appliqué piece the same distance from the edge as the turning allowance.

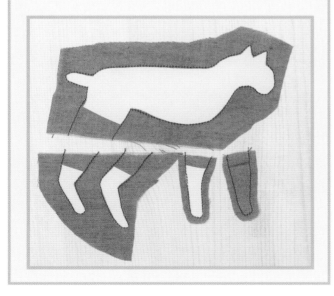

Bonded appliqué

This very quick appliqué method involves ironing fusible web to the back of the fabric, cutting out the pieces and ironing them onto a backing fabric so the webbing bonds them together.

- Bonded appliqué is suitable for fine details.

- Because the appliqué is bonded to the background, any seams in the background fabric will make the appliqué lumpy, so simplify the block with a single piece of fabric for the background.

- As with freezer paper appliqué, the appliqué shapes need to be traced as mirror images onto the back of the fusible web paper. With this method the appliqué pieces need no turning allowance.

- There are various brands of fusible web available, so follow the manufacturer's instructions for specific bonding times and temperatures.

- Fusible web stiffens fabrics and can make hand sewing difficult, so the edges of the bonded motif are best machine stitched with a zigzag or blanket stitch, or just several lines of straight stitch.

Bonded appliqué can cause shadowing problems if the appliqué fabric is not dense enough to block strong contrasts in the background design, like the stripes shown here, so select fabrics with care when using this technique.

Joining the blocks

Unless you are making a series of small coasters, pincushions or similar projects from your blocks, you will need to join blocks together. The original coverlet blocks are joined in the same way as they were made, by oversewing. The coverlet was most likely joined together in sections starting from the centre outwards, as most patchworks of that era seem to have been made as a medallion. This would be the easiest method to organize the blocks too.

- For machine patchwork and assembling hand appliquéd blocks by machine, the blocks can be sewn together in a combination of units and strips.

- If you have used mosaic patchwork for your project, you may remove the papers once the blocks are joined, but for a true replica, the papers should stay inside the coverlet.

- Unless you have set out to recreate the original coverlet layout, you will probably want to try out several different arrangements for your blocks – a digital camera can be very useful for this. The original coverlet has no sashing and adding strips between the blocks would change the appearance from an overall mosaic of pieces to a sampler quilt, but sashing could be added if you wish.

- Without sashing, there is the issue of which way to press the seams between the blocks. If you intend to finish your project as a coverlet and not to add wadding (batting), the seams between the blocks could be pressed open. If you want to quilt it, these seams are better pressed to one side, in alternate directions between rows of blocks, giving a ditch so there is somewhere to quilt. You will need to experiment with seam pressing directions as, depending on the construction of two adjacent blocks, some seams will naturally lie to one side more easily than the other. If the seams are pressed open, any quilting between the blocks would sit on the seam stitches only, with no fabric beneath.

Adding a border

Evidence suggests that the original coverlet had a border, now removed. We have no way of knowing what this would have looked like, but it is possible that the border may have been either plain or pieced.

If you choose to add a pieced border, consider the orientation of the blocks. It is fairly clear that the coverlet in its current form must have covered the top of the bed and not draped down at the sides, as blocks such as Pattern 37 (original block 81) would have been the wrong way round. Several other slightly later 18th-century coverlets have wide borders on the sides and bottom edge, with a narrower border at the top and square 'cut outs' at the bottom corners, presumably for bedposts. There are several surviving sets of patchwork bed drapes (curtains and pelmets) from later in the century, which would give scope for another approach to using the blocks, perhaps as a headboard or bedhead wall hanging.

This picture shows the back of a panel made by Pauline Adams, created from blocks made by members of the replica project team, using the original mosaic patchwork technique.

Backing the patchwork

The linen backing on the coverlet was pieced from several items, including monogrammed linen undergarments. If you want to make a historical recreation, this could be substituted with a linen sheet, as in the replica coverlet. An interlining of cotton flannel or similar interlining would help to support the patchwork and give the piece a little extra body, and it could be lightly hand quilted along the joins between the blocks. At some point it is thought to have had another backing, possibly green, as there are remnants of green silk thread outlining the

blocks on the back, so this is another historically inspired backing option. The backing and wadding (batting) or interlining need to be approximately 2in (5cm) larger than the patchwork all round. Make a quilt sandwich with the backing face down, the interlining on top of the backing and the patchwork on top. There are various ways to prepare the quilt sandwich for quilting, so use your favourite method. If you have used silk fabrics, tacking (basting) with thread or pins will probably mark them, so try tacking with thread along the seam lines and remove this as you quilt.

The original coverlet was backed with recycled linen, including items of clothing, some monogrammed with the same initials as the front of the coverlet – EH.

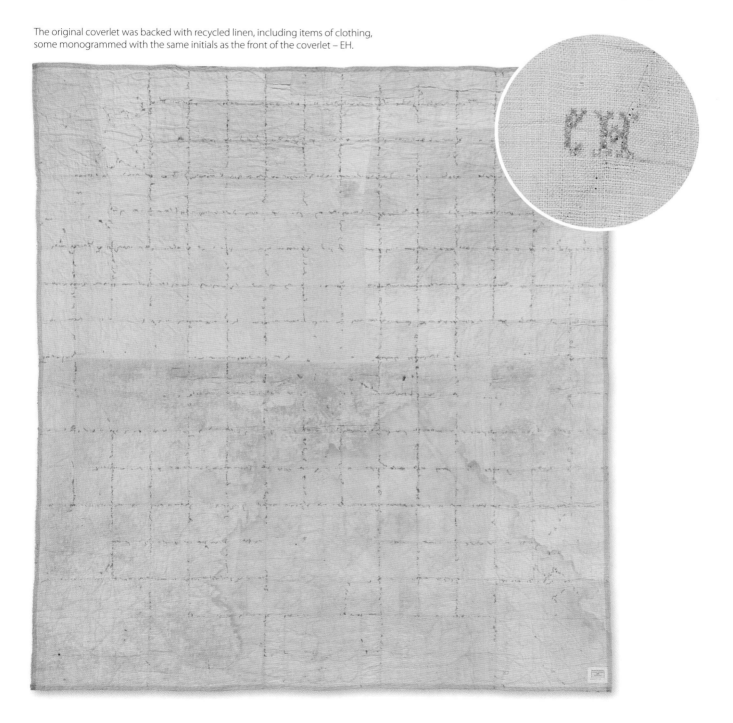

Simple quilting ideas

Fragments of silk stitching indicate that the coverlet may have had another backing at some point, but there is no evidence that it was ever quilted. Perhaps the green stitches were worked from the back, just to hold the (no longer present) backing in place. This does not mean you should not quilt your patchwork, but think carefully about where you quilt, as this is one instance where elaborate quilting could detract from the patchwork.

- Quilting in the ditch between all the blocks will probably suffice, with extra quilting around the motifs in the larger blocks, such as along the star edges in Patterns 48 and 49 or around the quatrefoil fleurs-de-lys in Patterns 1 and 63.

- Quilting in the ditch around the various block pieces and around motifs would anchor the wadding (batting) without interferring with the overall appearance too much, should extra quilting be desired.

- If you have used the original mosaic patchwork technique, every seam allowance will effectively be pressed open and at the point where the seams are sewn, there will be no fabric actually beneath the stitches, so your quilting would be through the stitches only.

- There are many excellent books devoted to the techniques of hand and machine quilting if you want to explore quilting ideas further.

Finishing the coverlet or quilt

British coverlets and quilts often have a knife-edge finish rather than a binding, like modern quilts. Of course, you could use a standard double-fold binding if you wish, or complete your piece with a facing.

1 To make a knife edge, cut the backing and wadding (batting) or interlining (if there is one) to the same size as the patchwork. If your patchwork is cotton, tack (baste) all around your work, about ½in (1.3cm) from the edge of the patchwork design, not the edge of the seam allowance. If there is wadding, separate the edges of the patchwork top and backing fabric and trim the wadding back to match the actual edge of the patchwork design, not the edge of the patchwork seam allowance, e.g., ⅜in (1cm) for mosaic patchwork and ¼in (6mm) for machine-sewn patchwork.

2 Turn in this seam allowance, i.e., ⅜in (1cm) or ¼in (6mm), all round the coverlet (or quilt, if there is wadding) – see Fig 1. Pin all round and slipstitch the edge of the patchwork to the edge of the backing. At each corner, fold in the seam allowances of the back and front of the coverlet in opposite directions and overlap them before tucking them in (Fig 2).

3 Quilt a line all around the coverlet as close to the edge as possible. Many traditional British quilts have a second line of quilting ¼in–⅜in (6mm–1cm) from the first, which helps give a firmer edge (although the coverlet does not have either).

Fig 1

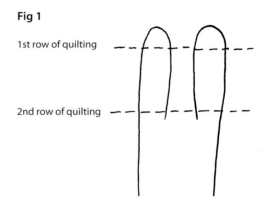

1st row of quilting

2nd row of quilting

Fig 2

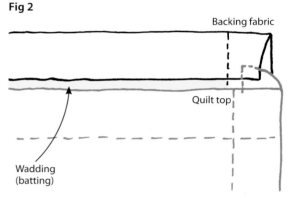

Backing fabric

Quilt top

Wadding (batting)

The lower left corner of the coverlet shows the very plain knife-edge finish.

Adding a label

A label will help people identify your work in the future. It can be as simple or as elaborate as you wish. Alas, the maker of the original 1718 coverlet did not label her work!

- Fine calico makes a good label or use any plain, light-coloured cotton.

- Try using a permanent acid-free pen to write directly on the label or embroider the information by hand or machine.

- Include your name, where the coverlet or quilt was made, the date and where the design came from.

- You could also add any other information you think would be of interest to your descendants or quilt historians of the future.

- Turn under the edges of the label and appliqué it to the back of your finished piece.

This small patchwork panel, combining Pattern 57, with several smaller blocks, was made by Tina Fenwick Smith using the original mosaic patchwork technique. You can experiment with adapting blocks with different or additional mosaic piecing seams, if you feel this would make blocks easier to sew.

BLOCK DIRECTORY

Pattern 1
(Original block 1)

This section describes and illustrates all of the blocks used in the 1718 coverlet. There are stepped instructions on making the blocks, pictures of the blocks and the templates needed to make them. The blocks are numbered, with the first pattern number indicating the modern numbering system used for this book. The original patchwork blocks are also given individual block numbers, as used for the replica project. These will be very useful if you are creating a reproduction of the original coverlet as you will be able to see the fabric types of colours used for specific blocks. All of the blocks are shown and labelled over the next few pages (not to scale). See also Layout of the Coverlet for a picture of the whole coverlet with these numbered blocks.

Pattern 5
(Original block 7)

The 'Original Method' instructions describe making the blocks using techniques the original maker would have used, that is, mosaic patchwork (sometimes called English paper piecing). So if you want to replicate the original coverlet, work from these instructions.

Pattern 8
(Original block 13)

The 'Modern Method' instructions describe making the blocks using techniques we use today, mostly machine patchwork and hand or machine appliqué. So if you want to make the coverlet using familiar techniques, or just a selection of blocks for projects of your own, follow these instructions.

Pattern 8
(Original block 19)

For both the original and modern methods, the instruction text is brief and needs to be read in conjunction with the Techniques section, so read the relevant instructions there before you start making a block. If you are aiming to make a faithful reproduction of the original coverlet and need advice on the fabric types and colours to use, read the section on Fabrics and Materials. Where the coverlet maker experimented by dividing up the paper template slightly differently for piecing each individual block, the easiest version was chosen for the pattern. Where the maker of the coverlet made more than one block using the same pattern but in different fabrics, we have included as many block pictures as the page space allows, so you can see the fabrics and colours.

Pattern 11
(Original block 25)

The templates are all given full size. For the larger blocks, a half or a quarter of the design is given full size, which can then be copied onto your fabric. Alternatively, the whole template is also shown at quarter size (25%), so if you prefer you can enlarge this on a photocopier by 400% to full size.

Pattern 14
(Original block 31)

Pattern 18
(Original block 37)

Pattern 2
(Original block 2)

Pattern 3
(Original block 3)

Pattern 4
(Original block 4)

Pattern 5
(Original block 5)

Pattern 6
(Original block 6)

Pattern 4
(Original block 8)

Pattern 3
(Original block 9)

Pattern 2
(Original block 10)

Pattern 1
(Original block 11)

Pattern 7
(Original block 12)

Pattern 3
(Original block 14)

Pattern 7
(Original block 15)

Pattern 9
(Original block 16)

Pattern 7
(Original block 17)

Pattern 3
(Original block 18)

Pattern 7
(Original block 20)

Pattern 10
(Original block 21)

Pattern 11
(Original block 22)

Pattern 8
(Original block 23)

Pattern 12
(Original block 24)

Pattern 12
(Original block 26)

Pattern 8
(Original block 27)

Pattern 11
(Original block 28)

Pattern 10
(Original block 29)

Pattern 13
(Original block 30)

Pattern 15
(Original block 32)

Pattern 16
(Original block 33)

Pattern 17
(Original block 34)

Pattern 18
(Original block 35)

Pattern 19
(Original block 36)

Pattern 17
(Original block 38)

Pattern 16
(Original block 39)

Pattern 15
(Original block 40)

Pattern 14
(Original block 41)

Pattern 13
(Original block 42)

Pattern 20
(Original block 43)

Pattern 21
(Original block 44)

Pattern 22
(Original block 45)

Pattern 23
(Original block 46)

Pattern 24
(Original block 47)

Pattern 25
(Original block 48)

Pattern 24
(Original block 49)

Pattern 23
(Original block 50)

Pattern 22
(Original block 51)

Pattern 21
(Original block 52)

Pattern 20
(Original block 53)

Pattern 26
(Original block 54)

Pattern 27
(Original block 55)

Pattern 28
(Original block 56)

Pattern 29
(Original block 57)

Pattern 30
(Original block 58)

Pattern 31
(Original block 59)

Pattern 32
(Original block 60)

Pattern 33
(Original block 61)

Pattern 34
(Original block 62)

Pattern 31
(Original block 63)

Pattern 30
(Original block 64)

Pattern 29
(Original block 65)

Pattern 28
(Original block 66)

Pattern 27
(Original block 67)

Pattern 26
(Original block 68)

Pattern 35
(Original block 69)

Pattern 36
(Original block 70)

Pattern 37
(Original block 71)

Pattern 38
(Original block 72)

Pattern 39
(Original block 73)

Pattern 40
(Original block 74)

Pattern 41
(Original block 75)

Pattern 42
(Original block 76)

Pattern 43
(Original block 77)

Pattern 40
(Original block 78)

Pattern 39
(Original block 79)

Pattern 38
(Original block 80)

Pattern 37
(Original block 81)

Pattern 36
(Original block 82)

Pattern 35
(Original block 83)

Pattern 38
(Original block 84)

Pattern 44
(Original block 85)

Pattern 44
(Original block 86)

Pattern 39
(Original block 87)

Pattern 45
(Original block 88)

Pattern 46
(Original block 89)

Pattern 46
(Original block 90)

Pattern 47
(Original block 91)

Pattern 39
(Original block 92)

Pattern 44
(Original block 93)

Pattern 44
(Original block 94)

Pattern 38
(Original block 95)

Pattern 11
(Original block 96)

Pattern 48
(Original block 97)

Pattern 30
(Original block 98)

Pattern 42
(Original block 99)

Pattern 49
(Original block 100)

Pattern 42
(Original block 101)

Pattern 30
(Original block 102)

Pattern 48
(Original block 103)

Pattern 11
(Original block 104)

Pattern 3
(Original block 105)

Pattern 44
(Original block 106)

Pattern 44
(Original block 107)

Pattern 39
(Original block 108)

Pattern 47
(Original block 109)

Pattern 46
(Original block 110)

Pattern 46
(Original block 111)

Pattern 45
(Original block 112)

Pattern 39
(Original block 113)

Pattern 44
(Original block 114)

Pattern 44
(Original block 115)

Pattern 3
(Original block 116)

Pattern 50
(Original block 117)

Pattern 51
(Original block 118)

Pattern 52
(Original block 119)

Pattern 39
(Original block 120)

Pattern 29
(Original block 121)

Pattern 40
(Original block 122)

Pattern 43
(Original block 123)

Pattern 42
(Original block 124)

Pattern 41
(Original block 125)

Pattern 40
(Original block 126)

Pattern 29
(Original block 127)

Pattern 39
(Original block 128)

Pattern 52
(Original block 129)

Pattern 51
(Original block 130)

Pattern 50
(Original block 131)

Pattern 6
(Original block 132)

Pattern 39
(Original block 133)

Pattern 53
(Original block 134)

Pattern 30
(Original block 135)

Pattern 3
(Original block 136)

Pattern 54
(Original block 137)

Pattern 55
(Original block 138)

Pattern 56
(Original block 139)

Pattern 3
(Original block 140)

Pattern 30
(Original block 141)

Pattern 53
(Original block 142)

Pattern 39
(Original block 143)

Pattern 6
(Original block 144)

Pattern 57
(Original block 145)

Pattern 58
(Original block 146)

Pattern 21
(Original block 147)

Pattern 59
(Original block 148)

Pattern 38
(Original block 149)

Pattern 44
(Original block 150)

Pattern 44
(Original block 151)

Pattern 38
(Original block 152)

Pattern 59
(Original block 153)

Pattern 21
(Original block 154)

Pattern 58
(Original block 155)

Pattern 57
(Original block 156)

Pattern 14
(Original block 157)

Pattern 60
(Original block 158)

Pattern 61
(Original block 159)

Pattern 62
(Original block 160)

Pattern 48
(Original block 161)

Pattern 62
(Original block 162)

Pattern 61
(Original block 163)

Pattern 60
(Original block 164)

Pattern 14
(Original block 165)

Pattern 63
(Original block 166)

Pattern 64
(Original block 167)

Pattern 65
(Original block 168)

Pattern 24
(Original block 169)

Pattern 44
(Original block 170)

Pattern 44
(Original block 171)

Pattern 24
(Original block 172)

Pattern 65
(Original block 173)

Pattern 64
(Original block 174)

Pattern 63
(Original block 175)

Pattern 66
(Original block 176)

Pattern 67
(Original
block 177)

Pattern 68
(Original block 178)

Pattern 67
(Original
block 179)

Pattern 66
(Original block 180)

Pattern 69
(Original
block 181)

Pattern 69
(Original
block 182)

A quatrefoil fleur-de-lys

Original patchwork blocks: 1 and 11

Block size: 13½in (34.3cm) square finished

Original method: mosaic patchwork

Modern method: machine patchwork and appliqué

Original Method

1 Make the quadruple fleur-de-lys. First, oversew the short seams linking the four fleurs-de-lys sections. Match balance lines throughout the block.

2 Insert the circle. Sew the gold flattened ovals to the patchwork.

3 Make the striped background, sewing the mitred corners first and then the pink strips.

4 Insert the fleur-de-lys into the background. For accurate points, sew each curved section from opposite ends, matching up points, indents and balance marks as you go and finishing in the centre of each section with a few stitches overlapping.

Modern Method

1 Make the block background first. Fussy cut eight $7^3/_{16}$in x $3^1/_{16}$in (18.3cm x 7.8cm) border strips from the blue and white stripe. Cut one end at 45 degrees – four sloping right and four left. Cut four $3^1/_{16}$in x $1^1/_8$in (7.8cm x 4.8cm) pink strips. Machine sew one striped piece to either side of each pink strip, to make four borders for the block. Cut one $8^7/_8$in (22.5cm) gold square (to give the illusion of the four ovals).

2 Assemble the block background, following the instructions for mitred squares (see Techniques: Machine Patchwork).

3 Cut four fleurs-de-lys, adding ¼in (6mm) seam allowance where they touch each other and appropriate turning allowance for your appliqué technique (see Techniques: Appliqué). Join and appliqué the fleur-de-lys, aligning the points on the background mitres and on the edge of the gold square, to create the ovals.

4 Cut a $3^7/_8$in (9.8cm) diameter circle, add the turning allowance and appliqué to the centre.

For a simplified appliqué-only block, omit the patchwork background and cut a 14in (35.5cm) square instead.

Fig 1

Whole block (25% size – enlarge by 400%)

Fig 1 shows the whole block reduced in scale and Fig 2 shows a quarter of the template at full size. Follow the instructions with the template.

Fig 2
Template (quarter)
Actual size of whole template 13½in (34.3cm) square

Fold a 13½in (34.3cm) paper square into quarters and trace off the template, lining up along the folds as indicated by the dashed lines. Repeat the design for the three other quarters by tracing or carefully cut out the pattern through all the layers with the paper still folded. Draw balance marks across each seam line to match up the fleur-de-lys quarters with the correct border sections (see Techniques: Mosaic Patchwork).

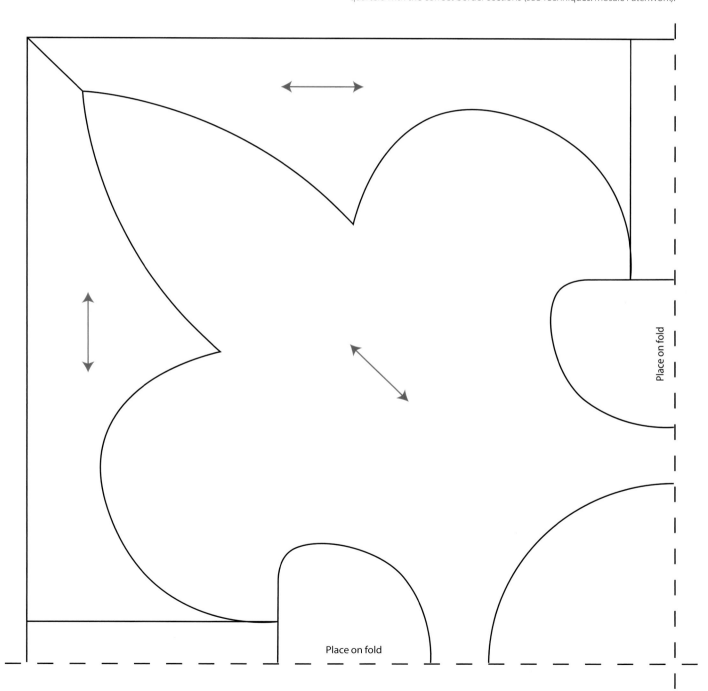

Place on fold

Place on fold

A quatrefoil fleur-de-lys

A framed square

Original patchwork blocks: 2 and 10

Block size: 4½in (11.4cm) square finished

Original method: mosaic patchwork

Modern method: machine patchwork

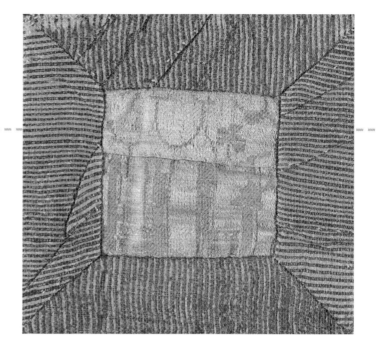

Original Method

1 Cut out and tack (baste) all pieces.
2 Oversew each frame section to the centre square. Match balance lines throughout the block.
3 Sew each mitre in turn, starting at the outside of the point and sewing towards the centre.

Modern Method

1 Use one of the identical frame border templates to cut all four border pieces from a 1⅝in (4.2cm) strip, adding a ¼in (6mm) seam to each (see Techniques: Rotary Cutting with Templates).
2 Cut a 2¾in (7cm) centre square.
3 Assemble the block, following the instructions for mitred squares (Techniques: Machine Piecing Mitres).

Fig 1
Template
Actual size 4½in (11.4cm) square

This is the whole block at full size. Arrows indicate directions of fabric stripes. Draw balance marks across each seam line (see Techniques: Mosaic Patchwork).

A diagonally quartered square

Original patchwork blocks: 3, 9, 14, 18, 105, 116, 136, 140

Block size: 4½in (11.4cm) square finished

Original method: mosaic patchwork

Modern method: machine patchwork

Original Method

1 Cut out and tack (baste) all pieces.
2 Oversew the triangles together in pairs, sewing from the block corners towards the centre. Match balance lines throughout the block.

Modern Method

1 Use one of the identical triangle templates to cut two triangles from each fabric, cutting from a 2⅞in (7.3cm) wide strip and adding a ¼in (6mm) seam to each piece (see Techniques: Rotary Cutting with Templates).
2 Assemble the block, sewing the triangles together in pairs and then sewing the pairs together.

TIP
Line up the fabric stripes as per the original block.

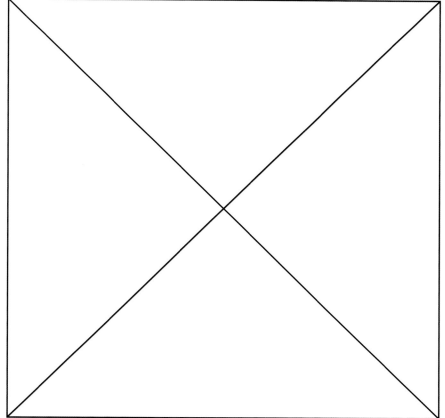

Fig 1
Template
Actual size 4½in (11.4cm) square
This is the whole block at full size.
Draw balance marks across each seam line
(see Techniques: Mosaic Patchwork).

A cross

Original patchwork blocks: 4, 8

Block size: 4½in (11.4cm) square finished

Original method: mosaic patchwork

Modern method: machine patchwork

Original Method

1 Cut out and tack (baste) all pieces.
2 Oversew one square on either side of the shorter strips, then join these pieces with the longer strip, sewing from the strip ends towards the centre. Take care to position the blue and green squares as diagonal opposites for the three-fabric version and to match up the strip on each side of the cross as it passes through the centre point.

Modern Method

1 Cut four 2⅜in (6cm) squares for the corners, two 2⅜in x 1¼in (6cm x 3.2cm) strips and one 5in x 1¼in (12.7cm x 3.2cm) strip for the cross.
2 Sew a square on either side of a short strip, and repeat to make two units. Sew the long strip between the two units to complete the block.

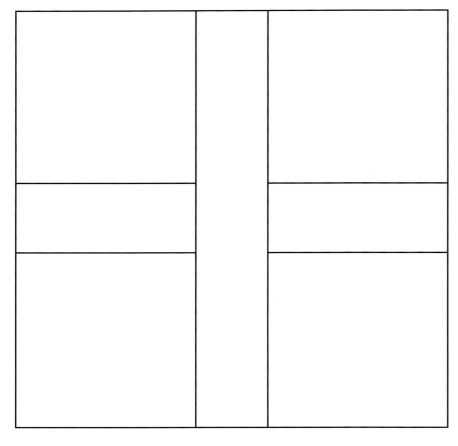

Fig 1
Template
Actual size 4½in (11.4cm) square
This is the whole block at full size. Draw balance marks across each seam line (see Techniques: Mosaic Patchwork).

A small framed square

Original patchwork blocks: 5, 7

Block size: 4½in (11.4cm) square finished

Original method: mosaic patchwork

Modern method: machine patchwork

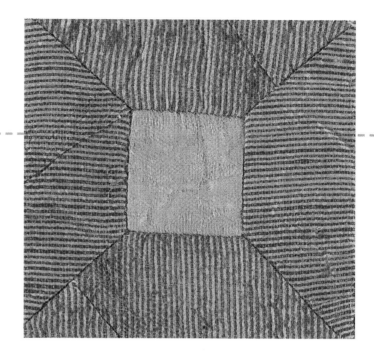

Original Method

1 Cut out and tack (baste) all pieces.
2 First, oversew the each frame section to the centre square. Match balance lines throughout the block.
3 Sew each mitre in turn, starting at the outside of the point and sewing towards the centre.

Modern Method

1 Use one of the identical frame border templates to cut all four border strips from a 2in (5cm) wide strip, adding a ¼in (6mm) seam to each (see Techniques: Rotary Cutting with Templates).
2 Cut a 2in (5cm) centre square.
3 Assemble the block, following the instructions for mitred squares (see Techniques: Machine Piecing Mitres).

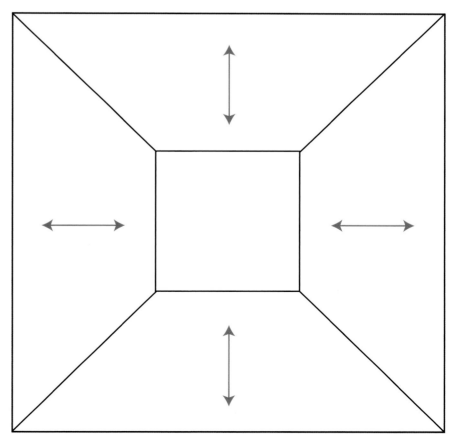

Fig 1
Template
Actual size 4½in (11.4cm) square
This is the whole block at full size. Arrows indicate the direction of the fabric stripe. Draw balance marks across each seam line (see Techniques: Mosaic Patchwork).

A pointed fleur-de-lys variation

Original patchwork blocks: 6, 132, 144

Block size: 4½in (11.4cm) square finished

Original method: mosaic patchwork

Modern method: machine patchwork and appliqué

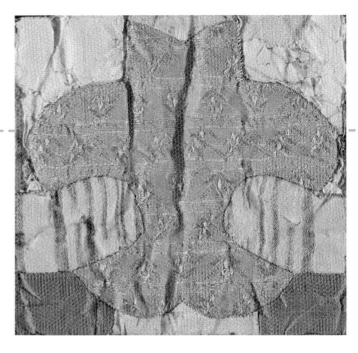

Pattern 6 is one of several unusual designs similar to a fleur-de-lys. Their exact origin or meaning is unknown – were they obscure badges or heraldic inspirations, motifs from the maker's local architecture or household or just symmetrical shapes invented by the maker during paper cutting?

Original Method

1 Cut out and tack (baste) all pieces. Assemble the block in sections. Match balance lines throughout the block. Sew the top centre yellow piece to the top of the fleur-de-lys.
2 Sew the upper corners to the fleur-de-lys, then the striped side pieces, matching the balance marks carefully around the curves.
3 Sew the bottom yellow piece to the blue corners, and then sew this completed blue/yellow piece to the bottom of the fleur-de-lys.

Modern Method

1 Cut a 5in (12.7cm) square from the fabric you want to show at the centre top and the centre bottom of the block.
2 Using the templates from Fig 1, cut the corners and side pieces (the blue stripe and the blue and pink), with an extra ¼in (6mm) allowance all round. Refer to Techniques: Appliqué for a choice of appliqué techniques, including needle-turn appliqué and freezer paper appliqué.
3 Pin the side pieces to the backing square. Turn under a ¼in (6mm) hem on the corner pieces where they overlap the side pieces and the background square at the top and bottom, but leave the other edges raw. Pin in place and appliqué the turned-under edges.
4 Adding the appropriate turning allowance for your chosen appliqué technique, cut out the fleur-de-lys as shown in Fig 1 and appliqué it to the block centre to finish the block.

For a simplified block, replace the pieced background with a 5in (12.7cm) square – try a large-scale plaid or check.

TIP

A modern dobby weave (such as a Japanese taupe with a woven texture), a subtle stripe or a small tone-on-tone print would all make good alternatives for the fleur-de-lys motif. Take care to keep the points sharp if using an appliqué technique with slightly thicker materials, such as taupe woven fabrics.

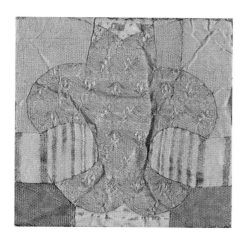
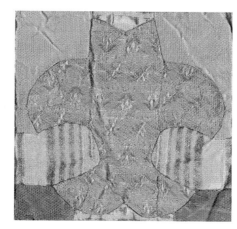

In Pattern 6 (original blocks 6, 132 and 144) a silvery grey dobby weave silk is used for the fleur-de-lys against a background of two solid blues (the same blue stripe as Pattern 1) and yellow ochre at the top and bottom centre. Each of the three blocks appears identical, although the block used at the top of the quilt seems to have had another stripe used for the upper corners, now worn away.

Fig 1
Template
Actual size 4½in (11.4cm) square

Fig 1 shows the whole block. Arrows indicate fabric stripe direction. Draw balance marks across each seam line (see Techniques: Mosaic Patchwork).

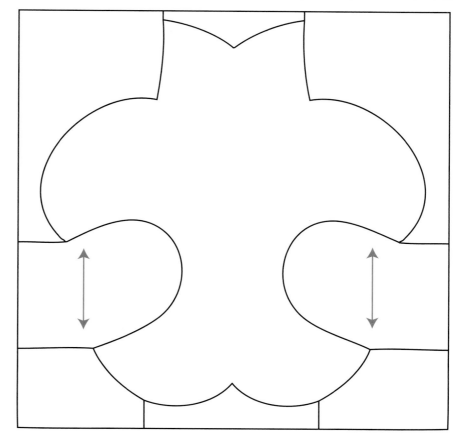

A large square with cornerstones

Original patchwork blocks: 12, 15, 17, 20

Block size: 4½in (11.4cm) square finished

Original method: mosaic patchwork

Modern method: machine patchwork

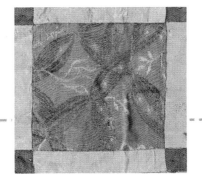 

Original Method

1 Cut out and tack (baste) all pieces.

2 Oversew two border strips to opposite sides of the centre square.

3 Sew one cornerstone square to each end of two remaining border strips, then sew these to the block centre, lining up the corner squares.

TIP

Try a print or batik for an alternative to the woven brocade used for original blocks 12 and 20.

Modern Method

1 Cut four 1⅛in (2.9cm) squares for the cornerstones, four 3¾in x 1⅛in (9.5cm x 2.9cm) border strips and one 3¾in (9.5cm) centre square.

2 Sew a border strip to opposite sides of the centre square.

3 Sew one cornerstone square to each end of two remaining border strips, and then sew these units to the top and bottom of the block.

Fig 1
Template
Actual size 4½in (11.4cm) square

This is the whole block at full size. Draw balance marks across each seam line (see Techniques: Mosaic Patchwork).

Four squares

Original patchwork blocks: 13, 19, 23, 27

Block size: 4½in (11.4cm) square finished

Original method: mosaic patchwork

Modern method: machine patchwork

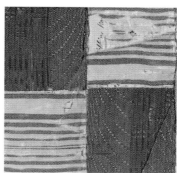

Original Method

1 Cut out and tack (baste) all pieces.
2 Oversew the squares together in pairs, and then sew the pairs together to make the block.

Modern Method

1 Cut four 2¾in (7cm) squares.
2 Machine sew the squares together in pairs, and then sew the pairs together, aligning the fabric stripes correctly.

TIP
Line up the fabric stripes as seen in the original blocks.

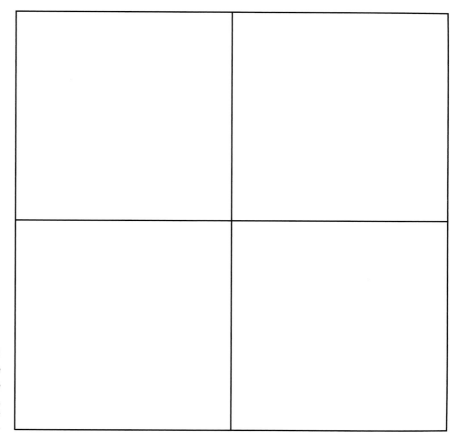

Fig 1
Template
Actual size 4½in (11.4cm) square
This is the whole block at full size.
Draw balance marks across each seam line
(see Techniques: Mosaic Patchwork).

Nine squares with striped centre

Original patchwork block: 16

Block size: 4½in (11.4cm) square finished

Original method: mosaic patchwork

Modern method: machine patchwork

Original Method

1 Cut out and tack (baste) all pieces.

2 Fussy cut the centre triangles so the stripes will match up. Oversew the triangles together in pairs to make the centre square.

3 Sew two border strips to opposite sides of the centre square.

4 Sew one cornerstone square to each end of the two remaining border strips, and then sew these to the block centre, lining up the corner squares.

Modern Method

1 Cut four 1⅝in (4.1cm) squares for the cornerstones and four strips each 1⅝in x 2¾in (4.1cm x 7cm).

2 Fussy cut four triangles for the centre from 1¾in (4.4cm) wide strip using the triangle template, adding a ¼in (6mm) seam allowance all round.

3 Machine sew the triangles together in pairs to make the centre square.

4 Sew two border strips to opposite sides of the centre square.

5 Sew one cornerstone square to each end of two remaining border strips, and then sew these to the block centre, lining up the corner squares.

Fig 1
Template
Actual size 4½in (11.4cm) square

This is the whole block at full size. Arrows indicate fabric stripe direction. Draw balance marks across each seam line (see Techniques: Mosaic Patchwork).

A curved star

Original patchwork block: 21, 29 (mirror image)

Block size: 4½in (11.4cm) square finished

Original method: mosaic patchwork

Modern method: appliqué

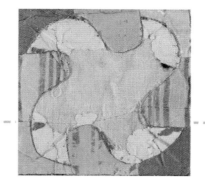
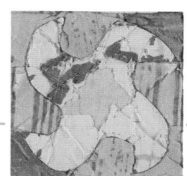

Original Method

1 Cut out and tack (baste) all pieces. Numbering the background pieces 1 to 9 and adding arrows to each piece to indicate right way up will help you sew the pieces together in the correct order.
2 Oversew each corner background piece to the next side piece, to create the continuous curve to fit to the side of the star.
3 Check the fit of each background section to the star and, matching the balance lines, sew each background section to the star.
4 Sew the remaining short seams from the outside of the block.

Modern Method

1 Cut a 5in (12.7cm) square, choosing the fabric you want to show at the centre top and bottom of the block.
2 Using the templates from Fig 1, cut the corners and side pieces (the blue, the pink and the blue stripe), with an extra ¼in (6mm) allowance all round. See Techniques: Appliqué for a choice of appliqué techniques, including needle-turn appliqué and freezer paper appliqué.
3 Pin the side pieces to the backing square. Turn under a ¼in (6mm) on the corner pieces where they overlap the side pieces but leave the other edges raw. Pin in place and appliqué the turned-under edges.
4 Adding the appropriate turning allowance for your appliqué technique, cut out the centre star as in Fig 1 and appliqué it to the block centre.

For a simplified block, replace the pieced background with a 5in (12.7cm) square – try a large-scale plaid or check.

Fig 1
Template
Actual size 4½in (11.4cm) square

This is the whole block at full size. Arrows indicate the direction of fabric stripes. Flip the template to make a mirror image of the design for a second block. Draw balance marks across each seam line (see Techniques: Mosaic Patchwork).

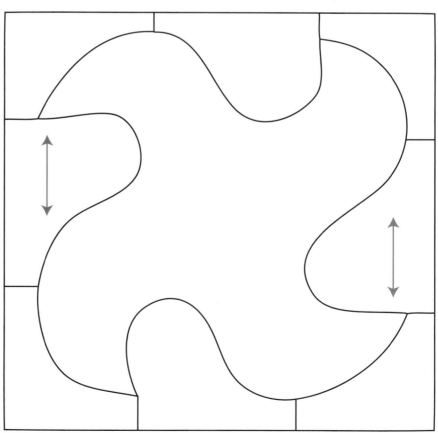

A curved star **65**

Nine squares

Original patchwork blocks: 22, 25, 28, 96,104

Block size: 4½in (11.4cm) square finished

Original method: mosaic patchwork

Modern method: machine patchwork

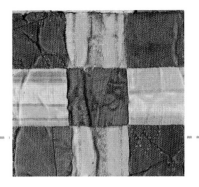

Original Method

1 Cut out and tack (baste) all pieces.
2 Oversew the squares together in strips of three and then sew the strips together to complete the block.

Fig 1
Template
Actual size 4½in (11.4cm) square

This is the whole block at full size. Arrows show the fabric stripe direction on original block 25. Draw balance marks across each seam line (see Techniques: Mosaic Patchwork).

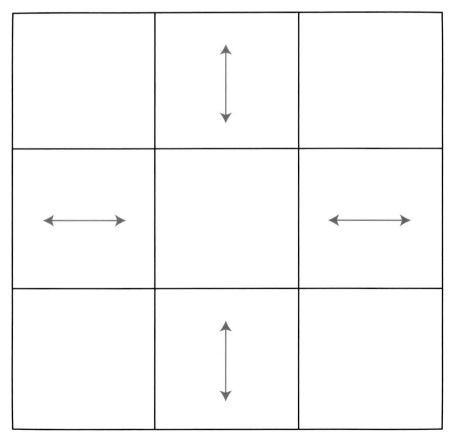

Modern Method

1 Cut nine 2in (5cm) squares from three, four or five different fabrics, depending on which version of the block you want to make.
2 Machine sew the squares together in strips of three and then sew the strips together to complete the block.

IDEA
Different versions of this simple block offer scope to play with stripes and directional fabrics, as the coverlet's maker did.

A framed square with cornerstones

Original patchwork blocks: 24, 26

Block size: 4½in (11.4cm) square finished

Original method: mosaic patchwork

Modern method: machine patchwork

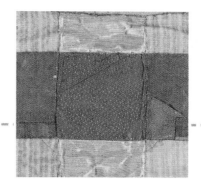

Original Method

1 Cut out and tack (baste) all pieces.

2 Oversew two border strips to opposite sides of the centre square.

3 Sew one cornerstone square to each end of two remaining border strips, and then sew these to the block centre to finish, lining up the corner squares.

Modern Method

1 Cut four 1⅝in (4.1cm) squares, four 1⅝in x 2¾in (4.1cm x 7cm) strips and one 2¾in (7cm) square.

2 Machine sew two border strips to opposite sides of the centre square.

3 Sew one cornerstone square to each end of two remaining border strips, and then finish the block by sewing these to the block centre, lining up the corner squares.

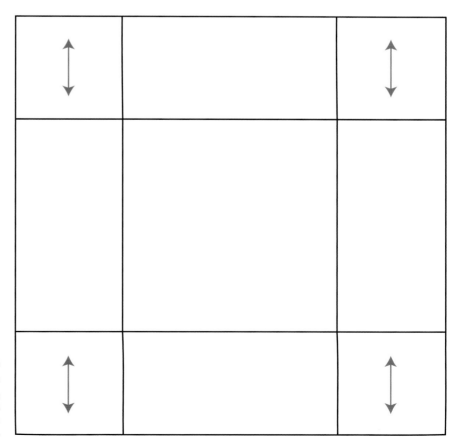

Fig 1
Template
Actual size 4½in (11.4cm) square
This is the whole block at full size. Arrows show fabric stripe directions on original block 24. Draw balance marks across each seam line (see Techniques: Mosaic Patchwork).

Birds and bells

Original patchwork blocks: 30, 42

Block size: 9in (22.9cm) square finished

Original method: mosaic patchwork

Modern method: appliqué

Original Method

1 Cut out and tack (baste) all pieces. Assemble the block in sections. Oversew the corner pieces to the tails of each bird and complete each bird section by sewing the pieces between the wings and body.

2 Sew the bell handles to each bell. Sew one bell section to each bird section to make four units.

3 Sew the units together in pairs and then sew the pairs together to finish.

Modern Method

1 Cut a 9½in (24.1cm) square for the block background, choosing the main fabric you want in the block corners, e.g., the green.

2 Cut four bells with an extra ¼in (6mm) allowance all round. Turn under ¼in (6mm) at each end of the bell rim but leave the remaining allowances unturned. Position each bell centrally on each side of the background square, lining up the straight bottom edge of the bell with the edge of the background square. Tack (baste) in place and appliqué the turned-under ends to the background (see Techniques: Appliqué).

3 Cut one 2⅝in (6.7cm) square for the bell handles, turn ¼in (6mm) under all round and press. Appliqué this to the centre of the block.

4 Adding the appropriate turning allowance for your appliqué technique, cut out four birds. Position as shown in Fig 1 and pin in place.

5 Cut four pieces from the corner templates in Fig 2 (the pieces just behind the birds' tails) adding a ¼in (6mm) all round. Position these in the block corners, so the edges line up with the edge of the square. Turn under the sides to continue the line of the birds' tails, tucking the inner edge under the tails.

6 Appliqué the birds and the corner pieces to complete the block.

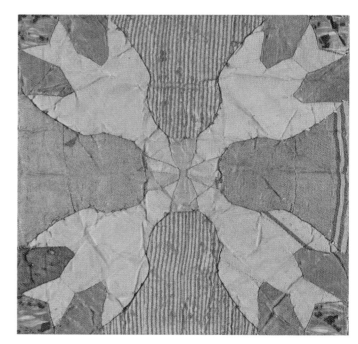

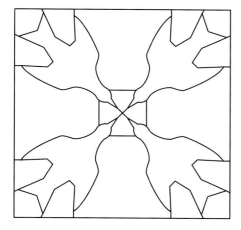

Fig 1
Whole block (25% size) – enlarge by 400%

Fig 1 shows the whole block reduced in scale and Fig 2 shows a quarter of the template at full size. Follow the instructions with the template.

IDEA
The original block uses a wide stripe to suggest the bell rim – you could get a similar effect by adding a narrow striped strip along the edge of the bell piece.

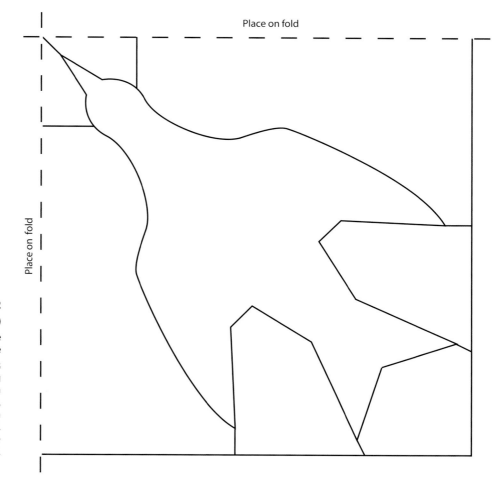

Place on fold

Place on fold

Fig 2
Template (quarter of design)
Actual size of whole template
9in (22.9cm) square

Fold a 9in (22.9cm) paper square into quarters and trace off the template, lining up along the folds as indicated. Repeat the design for the other three quarters by tracing, or carefully cut out the pattern through all the layers with the paper still folded. Draw balance marks across each seam line (see Techniques: Mosaic Patchwork).

An acorn or club shape

Original patchwork blocks: 31, 41,157, 165

Block size: 4½in (11.4cm) square finished

Original method: mosaic patchwork

Modern method: machine patchwork and appliqué

Original Method

1 Cut out and tack (baste) all pieces.
2 Assemble the block in sections. Match balance lines throughout the block.
3 Sew the background together in sections to create a frame and insert the motif into the block centre.

Fig 1
Template
Actual size 4½in (11.4cm) square
Fig 1 shows the whole block. The arrow indicates the fabric stripe direction.
Draw balance marks across each seam line (see Techniques: Mosaic Patchwork).

Modern Method

1 Make the block background first. In pink, cut one 1⅝in (4.1cm) square, one 2¾in x 1⅝in (7cm x 4.1cm) strip and one 3⅞in x 1⅝in (9.8cm x 4.1cm) strip. In cream, cut one 2¾in (7cm) square and two 3⅞in x 1⅝in (9.8cm x 4.1cm) strips.
2 Border the cream square with pink strips on two sides, sewing the shorter pink strip first (see Fig 2). Sew the cream and pink 3⅞in (9.8cm) strips together and sew to the block. Sew the pink square to the remaining cream strip and add this to the block. The pink strips will form an 'L' shape in the block background, with the pink square in the block corner.
3 Appliqué the acorn motif, adding an appropriate turning allowance for your appliqué technique (see Techniques: Appliqué).
  For a simplified appliqué-only block, replace the pieced background with a 5in (12.7cm) square.

Fig 2

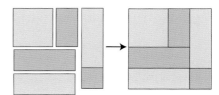

A horned fleur-de-lys

Original patchwork blocks: 32, 40

Block size: 4½in (11.4cm) square finished

Original method: mosaic patchwork

Modern method: appliqué

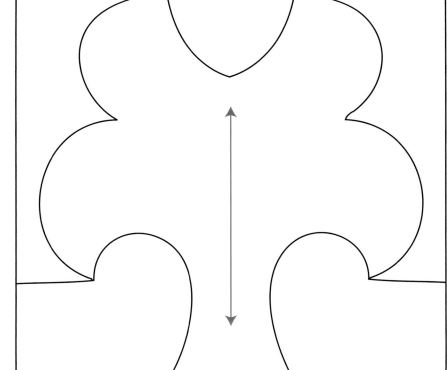

Original Method

1 Cut out and tack (baste) all pieces.
2 Start by sewing the V section to the top of the fleur-de-lys (see Techniques: Mosaic Patchwork). Match balance lines throughout the block.
3 Sew the remaining background together in sections to create the side pieces and then sew the motif between them.

Modern Method

1 Make the block background first. Cut a 5in (12.7cm) square from the main background fabric. Use the upper left and right of the block template to make background appliqué sections and cut these pieces with an extra ¼in (6mm) allowance all round (see Techniques: Appliqué). Line up the outside edge of these pieces with the top corners of the block and turn under a ¼in (6mm) to match the points of the fleur-de-lys, leaving the edges that will be overlapped by the fleur-de-lys raw. Pin and sew. Repeat for the lower corners.
2 Cut out the fleur-de-lys with an appropriate seam allowance and appliqué to the centre of the block, covering all the raw edges.

For a simplified block, you could omit the background appliqués.

Fig 1
Template
Actual size 4½in (11.4cm) square
Fig 1 shows the whole block. The arrow indicates the fabric stripe direction. Draw balance marks across each seam line (see Techniques: Mosaic Patchwork).

A double fleur-de-lys

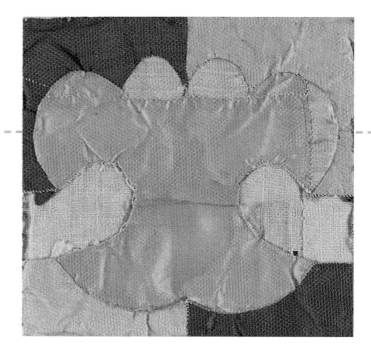

Original patchwork blocks: 33, 39

Block size: 4½in (11.4cm) square finished

Original method: mosaic patchwork

Modern method: appliqué

Original Method

1 Cut out and tack (baste) all pieces.

2 Start by sewing the centre top seam in the background pieces and sew to the fleur-de-lys.

3 Sew the side pieces to the fleur-de-lys. Repeat for the lower pieces to complete the block.

Fig 1
Template
Actual size 4½in (11.4cm) square

Fig 1 shows the whole block. Draw balance marks across each seam line (see Techniques: Mosaic Patchwork).

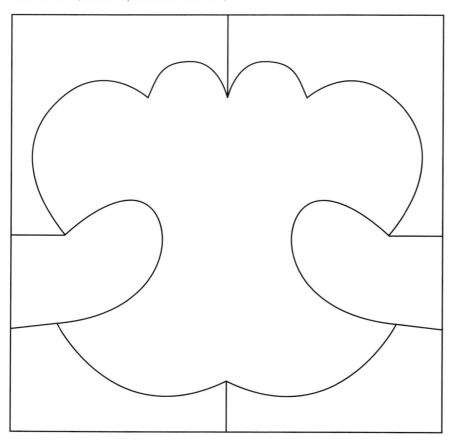

Modern Method

1 Make the block background first. Cut a 5in (12.7cm) square from the lightest background fabric for the block foundation. Use the upper left and lower right of the block template to make the purple background appliqué sections. Cut these pieces with an extra ¼in (6mm) allowance all round (see Techniques: Appliqué). Line up the outside edge of these pieces with the top left and bottom right corners of the block and turn under ¼in (6mm) at the centre top and bottom 'seams'.

2 Cut and appliqué the side pieces the same way, turning under the edges where they overlap the corner fabrics, but leaving raw the edges that will be overlapped by the fleur. Pin and sew.

3 Cut out the fleur with an appropriate seam allowance and appliqué to the centre of the block, covering raw edges of the upper corner pieces.

For a simplified block, omit the background appliqués or appliqué the fleur-de-lys onto Pattern 8.

A spiky fleur-de-lys

Original patchwork blocks: 34, 38

Block size: 4½in (11.4cm) square finished

Original method: mosaic patchwork

Modern method: machine patchwork and appliqué

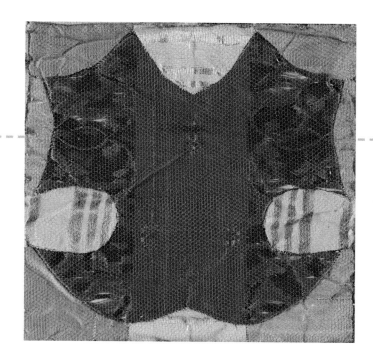

Original Method

1 Cut out and tack (baste) all pieces.

2 Start by sewing the V section to the top of the fleur-de-lys. Match balance lines throughout the block.

3 Sew the upper corners and then the side pieces to the fleur-de-lys.

4 Sew the bottom side seams in the remaining background pieces and sew to the fleur to finish.

Modern Method

1 Piece the block background from three strips – two 1⅞in x 5in (4.8cm x 12.7cm) blue stripe strips and one 2¼in x 5in (5.7cm x 12.7cm) gold strip. Use the template to cut four corner pieces with an extra ¼in (6mm) allowance all round (see Techniques: Appliqué).

2 Line up the outside edge of these corner pieces with the block corners and turn under ¼in (6mm) where the edges line up with the fleur-de-lys points, leaving the edges raw that will be overlapped by the fleur. Pin and sew.

3 Cut out the fleur-de-lys with an appropriate seam allowance and appliqué to the centre of the block, covering the raw edges of the corner pieces.

For a simplified block, you could omit the background appliqués.

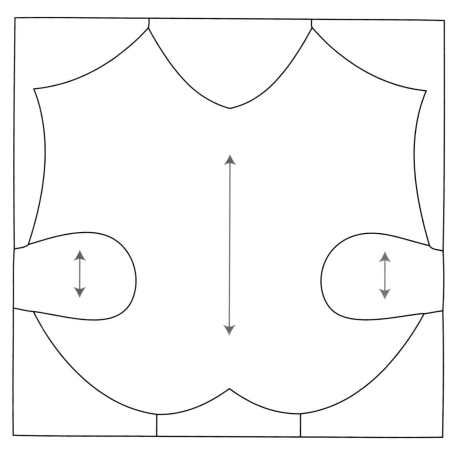

Fig 1
Template
Actual size 4½in (11.4cm) square

Fig 1 shows the whole block. Arrows indicate the fabric stripe direction. Draw balance marks across each seam line (see Techniques: Mosaic Patchwork).

A framed nine-patch

Original patchwork blocks: 35, 37

Block size: 4½in (11.4cm) square finished

Original method: mosaic patchwork

Modern method: machine patchwork

Original Method

1 Cut out and tack (baste) all pieces.

2 Sew corner squares on either side of the central side square. If the optional extra seams are added (shown as dashed lines in Fig 1), assemble the centre as a nine-patch, with the squares in strips of three (see Pattern 11). Match balance lines throughout the block.

3 Sew each mitre in turn, starting at the outside of the point and sewing towards the centre.

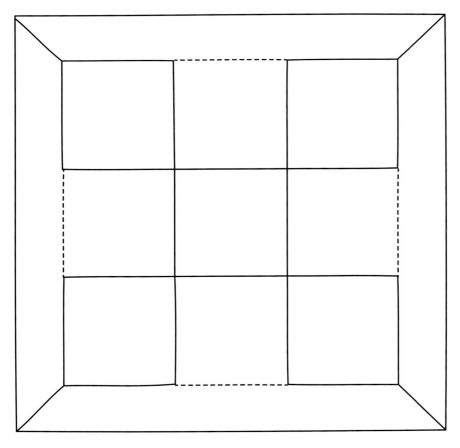

Modern Method

1 Make the block using the optional extra seams. Use one of the identical frame border templates to cut all four border strips from 1in x 5¾in (2.5cm x 14.6cm) strips, adding a ¼in (6mm) seam around the template.

2 Cut nine 1⁵⁄₃₂in (2.9cm) squares for the centre – these are easier to cut by adding a ¼in (6mm) all round the square templates than to measure 1⁵⁄₃₂in. Sew the squares together into a nine-patch unit.

3 Add the mitre strips to the block, following the instructions in Techniques: Machine Piecing Mitres.

Fig 1

Template

Actual size 4½in (11.4cm) square

This is the whole block at full size. Dashed lines show optional seams. Draw balance marks across each seam line (see Techniques: Mosaic Patchwork).

A heart

Original patchwork block: 36

Block size: 4½in (11.4cm) square finished

Original method: mosaic patchwork

Modern method: machine patchwork and appliqué

Original Method

1 Cut out and tack (baste) all pieces.

2 Sew the background triangles together, stitching from the outer corners inwards. Match balance lines throughout the block.

3 Sew the two heart pieces together and insert it into the centre of the block. Follow the tips in Techniques: Adapting Mosaic Patchwork about sewing sharp points to deal with the dip at the top of the heart.

Modern Method

1 Use one of the identical triangle templates from Pattern 3 to cut two triangles from each fabric, cutting from a 2⅞in (7.3cm) wide strip and adding a ¼in (6mm) seam to each piece.

2 Assemble the block, sewing the triangles together in pairs and then sewing the pairs together.

3 Sew the two heart pieces together and appliqué it into the centre of the block. Refer to Techniques: Appliqué for a choice of appliqué techniques, including needle-turn appliqué and freezer paper appliqué.

Fig 1
Template
Actual size 4½in (11.4cm) square
This is the whole block at full size. Draw balance marks across each seam line (see Techniques: Mosaic Patchwork).

A fleur-de-lys with dipped top

Original patchwork blocks: 43, 53

Block size: 4½in (11.4cm) square finished

Original method: mosaic patchwork

Modern method: machine patchwork and appliqué

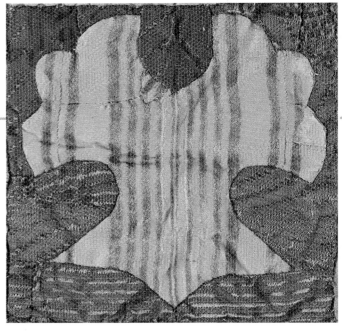

Original Method

1 Cut out and tack (baste) all pieces.
2 Start by sewing the V section to the top of the fleur-de-lys. Match balance lines throughout the block.
3 Sew the top corner pieces to the fleur-de-lys.
4 Sew the side pieces and the bottom strip to the fleur.

Fig 1
Template
Actual size 4½in (11.4cm) square
This is the whole block at full size. Arrows show the fabric stripe direction.
Draw balance marks across each seam line (see Techniques: Mosaic Patchwork).

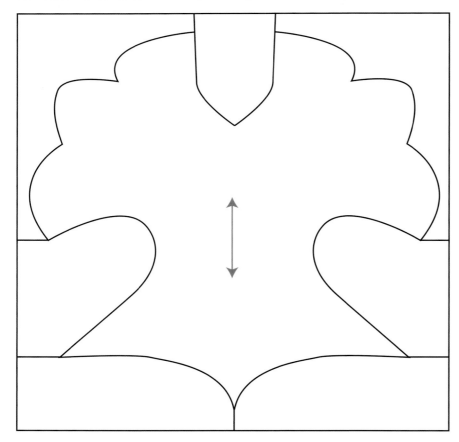

Modern Method

1 Cut a 5in (12.7cm) square, choosing the fabric you want to be at the centre top and bottom of the block.
2 Using the templates from Fig 1, cut the corners and side pieces with an extra ¼in (6mm) allowance all round (see Techniques: Appliqué).
3 Pin the side pieces to the backing square. Turn under a ¼in (6mm) at the bottom edge, but leave the other edges raw. Pin in place and appliqué the turned-under edges. Repeat for the upper corner pieces.
4 Cut out the fleur-de-lys with an appropriate seam allowance and appliqué to the centre of the block, covering the raw edges of the corner pieces.

The original block background was pieced from two very similar fabrics, but you could use a single piece for the background for a simplified block.

A square on point with split triangles

Original patchwork blocks: 44, 52, 147, 154

Block size: 4½in (11.4cm) square finished

Original method: mosaic patchwork

Modern method: machine patchwork

Original Method

1 Cut out and tack (baste) all pieces.
2 Oversew the inner triangles to the centre square.
3 Sew the outer triangles together in pairs, sewing inwards from the corner point.
4 Sew the corner units to the block centre. Match balance lines throughout the block.

Modern Method

1 Cut one 2¾in (7cm) square for the centre, two 3½in (8.9cm) squares in two different fabrics, quartered diagonally for the centre triangles, and four 2½in (6.4cm) squares halved diagonally for the outer triangles. Keep the two remaining triangles from each quartered 3½in (8.9cm) square to make a second block. Alternatively, use one of the identical triangle templates to cut two triangles from each fabric, cutting from a 1¾in (4.4cm) wide strip and adding a ¼in (6mm) seam allowance to each piece.
2 Sew the inner triangles to the sides of the centre square.
3 Sew the outer triangles together in pairs and then sew these corner units to the block centre.

Fig 1
Template
Actual size 4½in (11.4cm) square
This is the whole block at full size. Arrows show the fabric stripe direction on block 44. Draw balance marks across each seam line (see Techniques: Mosaic Patchwork).

A segmented circle

Original patchwork blocks: 45, 51

Block size: 4½in (11.4cm) square finished

Original method: mosaic patchwork

Modern method: machine patchwork

Original Method

1 Cut out and tack (baste) all pieces.

2 Oversew the circle segments together in pairs, taking care to line up the centre points. Sew one pair to each corner piece. Match balance lines throughout the block.

3 Sew the square units together in pairs, and then sew the pairs together to finish.

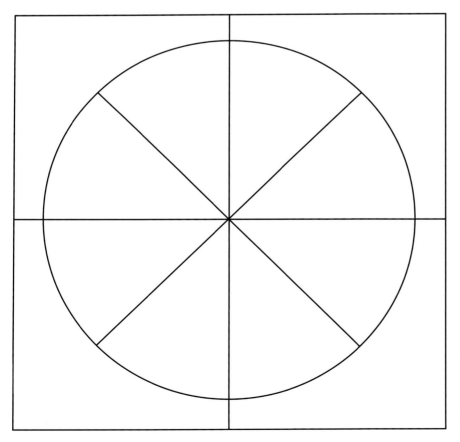

Modern Method

1 Cut all pieces using the templates in Fig 1, adding a ¼in (6mm) all round.

2 Machine sew the circle segments together in pairs, taking care to line up the centre points. Sew one pair to each corner piece with a curved seam, sewing with the concave curve of the corner piece on top, easing it to the convex segment.

3 Sew the square units together in pairs and then sew the pairs together to finish the block.

Fig 1
Template
Actual size 4½in (11.4cm) square

This is the whole block at full size.
Draw balance marks across each seam line
(see Techniques: Mosaic Patchwork).

A hinge shape

Original patchwork blocks: 46, 50

Block size: 4½in (11.4cm) square finished

Original method: mosaic patchwork

Modern method: appliqué

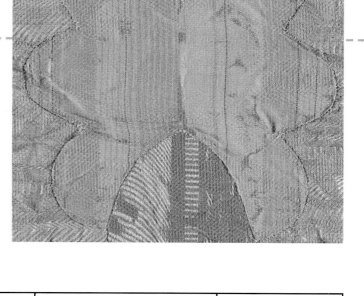

Original Method

1 Cut out and tack (baste) all pieces.

2 Start by sewing the side pieces to the hinge. Match balance lines throughout the block.

3 Sew the centre top and centre bottom background sections to each end of the hinge shape.

Modern Method

1 Cut one 5in (12.7cm) square of fabric for the background.

2 Cut out the fleur-de-lys with an appropriate seam allowance and appliqué to the centre of the block. Refer to Techniques: Appliqué for a choice of appliqué techniques, including needle-turn appliqué and freezer paper appliqué.

TIP
The original silk used for the hinge shape has a subtle stripe, so line up the striped fabric as shown in the original block.

Fig 1
Template
Actual size 4½in (11.4cm) square
Fig 1 shows the whole block.
Draw balance marks across each seam line
(see Techniques: Mosaic Patchwork).

A triangle-square on point

Original patchwork blocks: 47, 49, 169, 172

Block size: 4½in (11.4cm) square finished

Original method: mosaic patchwork

Modern method: machine patchwork

Original Method

1 Cut out and tack (baste) all pieces.
2 Oversew the inner triangles together
to make a triangle square.
3 Sew the corner triangles to the block centre.
Match balance lines throughout the block.

Fig 1
Template
Actual size 4½in (11.4cm) square

This is the whole block at full size. Draw balance marks across
each seam line (see Techniques: Mosaic Patchwork).

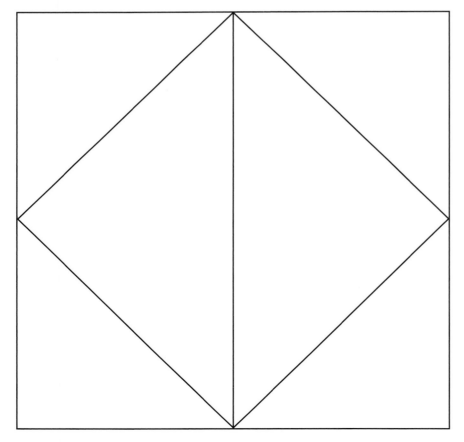

Modern Method

1 Cut two 4^{1}/$_{16}$in (10.3cm) squares
halved diagonally for the centre
triangles and cut two 3^{1}/$_{8}$in (7.9cm)
squares halved diagonally for the
corner triangles. Keep the two
remaining centre triangles from
each quartered 4^{1}/$_{16}$in (10.3cm)
square to make a second block.
2 Machine sew the inner triangles
together to make a triangle-square.
3 Sew the corner triangles to
the block centre to finish.

Pattern **25** # Initials and date

Original patchwork block: 48

Block size: 4½in (11.4cm) square finished

Original method: mosaic patchwork

Modern method: appliqué

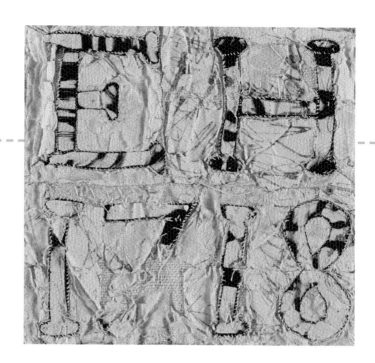

Original Method

1 Cut out and tack (baste) all pieces.
2 Oversew the letter serifs to the ends of the letters and the centre pieces to the '8' first. Match balance lines throughout the block.
3 Sew the top, centre and bottom bars of the 'E' and the centre bar of the 'H' to the background.
4 Now sew the rest of the letter and number pieces into position.
5 Sew the two halves of the block together to finish.

Modern Method

1 Cut one 5in (12.7cm) background square.
2 Cut out the individual letters and numbers, adding an appropriate turning allowance (see Techniques: Appliqué).
3 Use the templates provided for the letters and numbers. Appliqué the letters and numbers to the background. You may find it easier to cut the serifs separately for hemmed appliqué techniques and add these to the letters last. For bonded appliqué, cut each letter and number as a single piece without turning allowances.

Fig 1
EH 1718 Template
Actual size 4½in (11.4cm) square
This is the whole block at full size. Draw balance marks across each seam line (see Techniques: Mosaic Patchwork). See overleaf for the remaining letters and numbers.

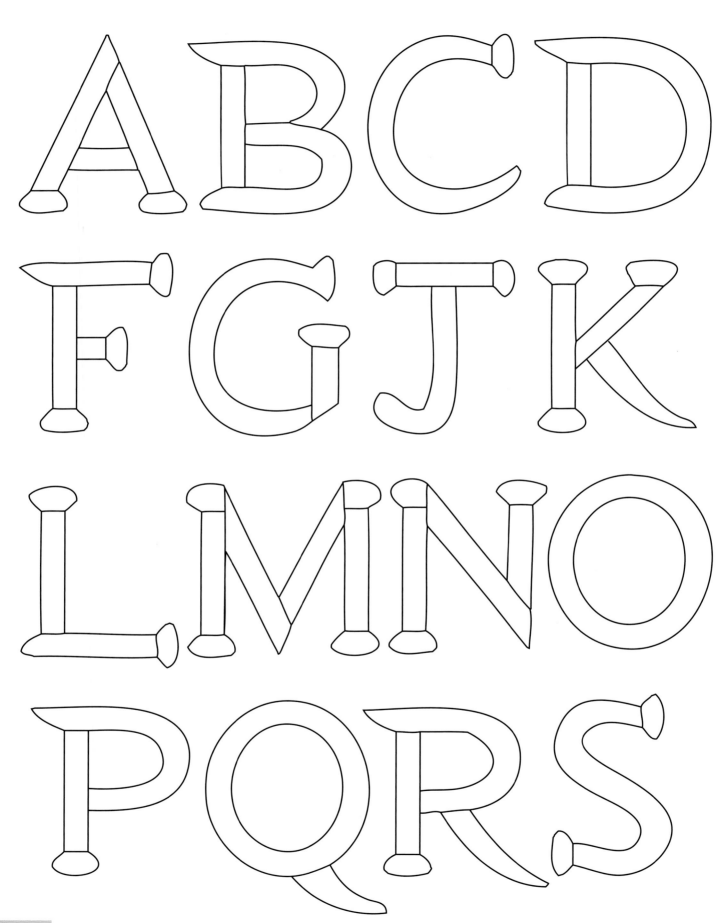

Fig 2
Alphabet and numbers templates (actual size)

Use these letters and numbers to create your own initials and date, or refer to the photograph of Block 25 to reproduce the original initials and date. E, H, 1, 7 and 8 are shown in Fig 1 and not included in Fig 2. Use the same template for number 1 and letter I.

Initials and date   **83**

Pattern 26

Pattern 26

Four circles and a diamond

Original patchwork blocks: 54, 68

Block size: 4½in (11.4cm) square finished

Original method: mosaic patchwork

Modern method: appliqué

Original Method

1 Cut out and tack (baste) all pieces.
2 Start by inserting the circles into the background. Match balance lines throughout the block.
3 Sew the diamond to the centre last.

Fig 1
Template
Actual size 4½in (11.4cm) square

Fig 1 shows the whole block. The arrow shows the fabric stripe direction in the centre. Draw balance marks across each seam line (see Techniques: Mosaic Patchwork).

Modern Method

1 Cut one 5in (12.7cm) square for the background.
2 Using the diamond template from Fig 1, cut out the centre piece adding a ¼in (6mm) seam allowance all round. Press the hem under and appliqué to the block centre. Refer to Techniques: Appliqué for a choice of appliqué techniques, including needle-turn appliqué and freezer paper appliqué.
3 Cut out the circles with an appropriate seam allowance and appliqué in position around the diamond to finish.

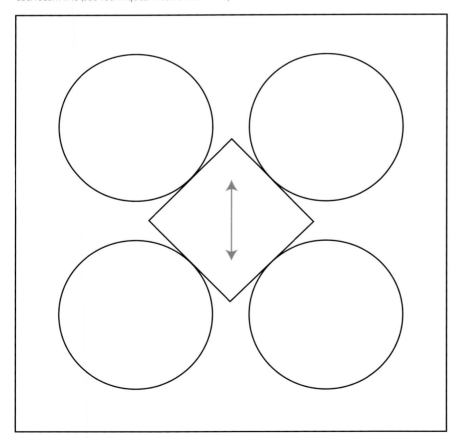

Sixteen squares

Original patchwork blocks: 55, 67

Block size: 4½in (11.4cm) square finished

Original method: mosaic patchwork

Modern method: machine patchwork

Original Method

1 Cut out and tack (baste) all pieces.

2 Oversew the squares together in pairs. Sew the pairs together into strips.

3 Sew the strips together make the block. Make sure stripes are aligned and that fabrics are placed correctly.

Modern Method

1 Cut sixteen 1⅝in (4.1cm) squares.

2 Machine sew the squares together in pairs, and then sew the pairs together into strips.

3 Sew the strips together to make the block. Make sure stripes are aligned and that fabrics are placed correctly.

TIP

The arrangement of squares has a subtle symmetry, both with fabric choice and the stripe direction. This is a very easy block to make, but check the patch layout carefully.

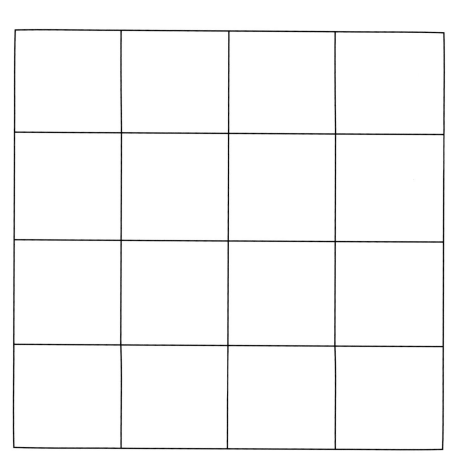

Fig 1
Template
Actual size 4½in (11.4cm) square
This is the whole block at full size. Draw balance marks across each seam line (see Techniques: Mosaic Patchwork).

A partridge

Original patchwork blocks: 56, 66 (mirror image)

Block size: 4½in (11.4cm) square finished

Original method: mosaic patchwork

Modern method: machine patchwork and appliqué

Original Method

1 Cut out and tack (baste) all pieces.

2 Sew the top diagonal background seams, starting at the block corners. Sew the head to the body and add the background piece to the tail (see tips on piecing sharp points in Techniques: Mosaic Piecing). Sew the small piece between the feet and sew to the lower background piece. Sew this to the remaining background piece.

3 Sew the two halves of the background together and insert the bird's body into the background. Embroider the eye (see Techniques: Embroidering Eyes).

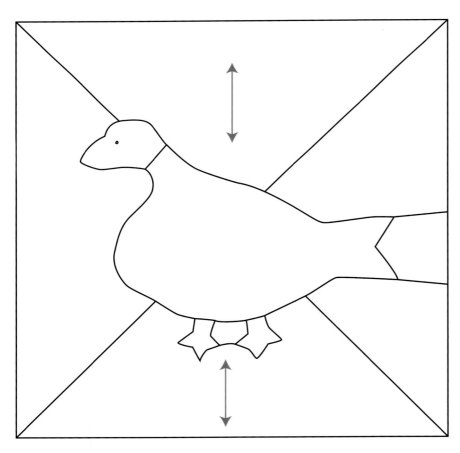

Modern Method

1 Make the background using one of the identical triangle templates from Pattern 3 to cut two triangles from each fabric, cutting from a 2⅞in (7.3cm) wide strip and adding a ¼in (6mm) seam to each piece.

2 Assemble the background, sewing the triangles together in pairs.

3 Cut out the bird's body, adding an appropriate seam allowance (see Techniques: Appliqué). The bird may be cut as a single piece. If it is cut as four pieces, as in original method, appliqué the feet first, then the body, then the head.

4 Embroider the eye to finish.

Fig 1
Template
Actual size 4½in (11.4cm) square

Fig 1 shows the whole block. Arrows indicate fabric stripe direction. Flip the template to make a mirror image of the design for a second block. Draw balance marks across each seam line (see Techniques: Mosaic Patchwork). The bird has been simplified by closing its beak, making it easier to sew, as was done for the replica coverlet.

Pattern 29

Four squares on point

Original patchwork blocks: 57, 65, 121, 127

Block size: 4½in (11.4cm) square finished

Original method: mosaic patchwork

Modern method: machine patchwork

Original Method

1 Cut out and tack (baste) all pieces.

2 Oversew the squares together in pairs and then join the pairs to make the block centre.

3 Sew the corner triangles to the block centre. Match balance lines throughout the block.

Modern Method

1 Cut four 2⅛in (5.4cm) squares for the centre. It is easier to cut these a little oversize and trim the four-patch centre later, or use the template to cut these, adding a ¼in (6mm) all round

2 Cut two 3⅛in (7.9cm) squares cut in half diagonally for the corner triangles.

3 Machine sew the squares together in pairs and then join the pairs to make the four-patch centre.

4 Trim the four-patch block to 3¹¹⁄₁₆in (8.1cm) before adding the corner triangles.

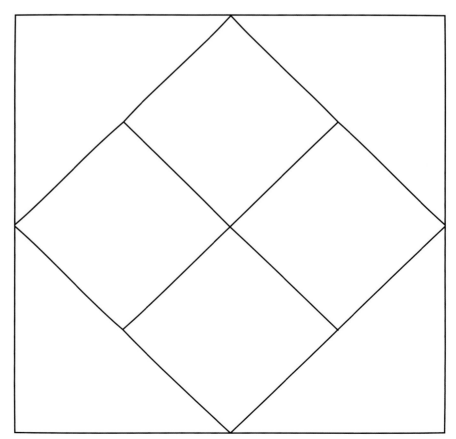

Fig 1
Template
Actual size 4½in (11.4cm) square
This is the whole block at full size.
Draw balance marks across each seam line
(see Techniques: Mosaic Patchwork).

A square on point

Original patchwork blocks: 58, 64, 98, 102, 135, 141

Block size: 4½in (11.4cm) square finished

Original method: mosaic patchwork

Modern method: machine patchwork

Original Method

1 Cut out and tack (baste) all pieces.
2 Oversew the corner triangles to the block centre. Match balance lines throughout the block.

Modern Method

1 Cut one 3⅝in (9.2cm) square for the centre.
2 Cut two 3⅛in (7.9cm) squares halved diagonally for the corner triangles (cut striped triangles individually from 2¼in/5.7cm strips).
3 Machine sew the corner triangles to the block centre.

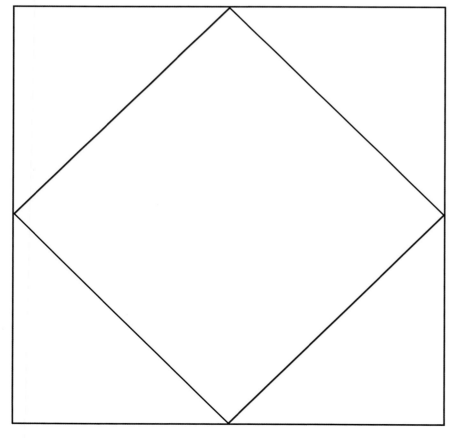

TIP
Use the template to cut striped triangles individually from a 2½in (5.7cm) strip, to ensure the stripes are travelling in the right direction in the block you are making.

Fig 1
Template
Actual size 4½in (11.4cm) square
This is the whole block at full size. Draw balance marks across each seam line (see Techniques: Mosaic Patchwork).

Five-squares cross on point

Original patchwork blocks: 59, 63

Block size: 4½in (11.4cm) square finished

Original method: mosaic patchwork

Modern method: machine patchwork

Original Method

1 Cut out and tack (baste) all pieces.
2 Oversew the pieces together to make three diagonal strips and then sew the strips together.
3 Add the last two corner triangles to finish the block. Match balance lines throughout the block.

Modern Method

1 Cut five 2⅛in (5.4cm) squares for the centre cross.
2 Cut two 2in (5cm) squares halved diagonally for the corner triangles and two 2½in (6.4cm) squares halved diagonally for the side triangles.
3 Machine sew the pieces together to make three diagonal strips and then sew the strips together.
4 Sew on the last two corner triangles to finish the block.

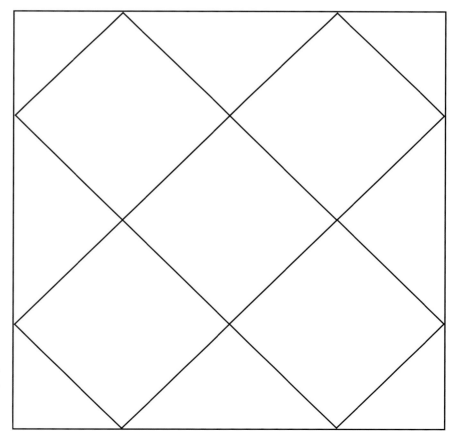

Fig 1
Template
Actual size 4½in (11.4cm) square
This is the whole block at full size.
Draw balance marks across each seam line
(see Techniques: Mosaic Patchwork).

A man

Original patchwork block: 60

Block size: 4½in (11.4cm) square finished

Original method: mosaic patchwork

Modern method: appliqué

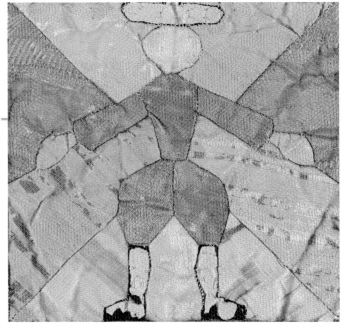

Original Method

1 Cut out and tack (baste) all pieces. Assemble the block in sections. Oversew the hat and head to the two pink upper background pieces. Sew the green background pieces to either side of the upper background section, lining up both ends carefully.

2 Sew the breeches together and sew lower legs to these. Sew the background piece between the legs and striped background pieces to either side of lower body.

3 Sew the body to the breeches at waist. Join hands and arms at the wrist and sew to yellow striped background pieces on each side. Sew all pieces together to finish.

Modern Method

1 Make the block background first. Add a turning allowance for your appliqué technique throughout. Cut a 5in (12.7cm) pink square. Using the upper part of the template, cut two pieces of green for top background, adding ¼in (6mm) allowance all round. Fold under ¼in (6mm) on left and right green diagonals and appliqué to the pink square.

2 Cut and appliqué the yellow stripe pieces the same way, leaving edges raw under the arms.

3 Cut bottom background piece as a triangle, adding ¼in (6mm) allowance.

4 Cut remaining pieces with turning allowances if required. Appliqué these, overlapping legs with breeches, hands with sleeves, head with hat, and then sleeves, breeches and neck with body.

Fig 1
Template
Actual size 4½in (11.4cm) square

This is the whole block at full size. Draw balance marks across each seam line (see Techniques: Mosaic Patchwork).

Four hearts

Original patchwork block: 61

Block size: 4½in (11.4cm) square finished

Original method: mosaic patchwork

Modern method: machine patchwork and appliqué

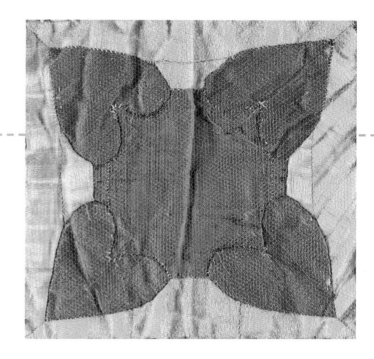

Original Method

1 Cut out and tack (baste) all pieces.
2 Oversew each border piece to the centre square – this will help you position the hearts. Match balance lines throughout the block.
3 Sew each heart, starting at the points.
4 Finish the block by sewing the short mitre seams from each corner inwards.

Modern Method

1 The background block is similar to Pattern 2. Cut one 3in (7.6cm) blue centre square. Cut four border pieces 1½in x 5¾in (3.8cm x 14.6cm) and trim the ends to 45 degrees.
2 Assemble the block in the same way as Pattern 2, following the instructions for mitred squares (Techniques: Machine Piecing Mitres).
3 Cut out four hearts, adding the appropriate turning allowance for your chosen appliqué technique, and appliqué to the block.

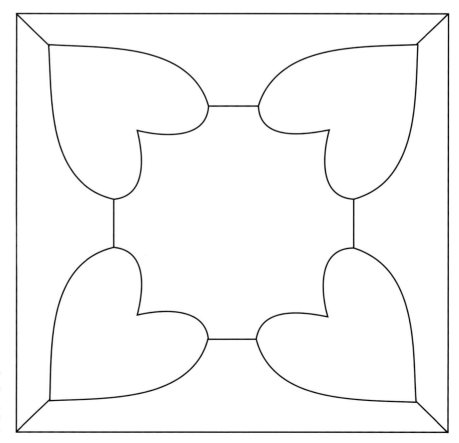

Fig 1
Template
Actual size 4½in (11.4cm) square
This is the whole block at full size. Draw balance marks across each seam line (see Techniques: Mosaic Patchwork).

A woman

Original patchwork block: 62

Block size: 4½in (11.4cm) square finished

Original method: mosaic patchwork

Modern method: appliqué

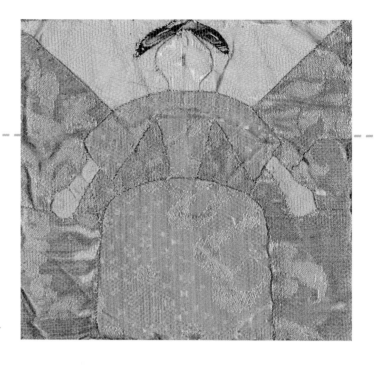

Original Method

1 Assemble the block in sections. Oversew the arms to the blue side background pieces and the head between the two pink upper background pieces.
2 Sew the hair/head to the top section. Sew the blue side pieces to the upper section, along the diagonals. Sew the lower blue background sections to the bodice sides and underside of the sleeves, stopping at lower point of sleeve. Sew the skirt into lower background, starting at bottom edge, towards centre. Sew the skirt in two steps from opposite sides.
3 Sew all pieces together to finish.

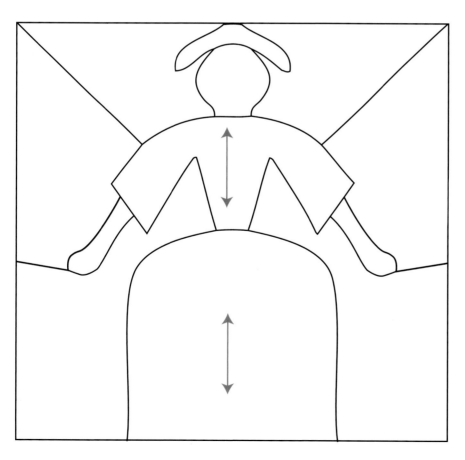

Modern Method

1 Make the block background first. Add the appropriate turning allowance. Cut a 5in (12.7cm) blue square. Using the upper part of template, cut a single piece of pink fabric for the top background, so it goes behind the head. Appliqué it to the blue square. Trim away excess blue fabric behind the pink.
2 Cut out the dress as two pieces, and then arms, head and hair. Temporarily pin the figure to the block, checking alignment of all pieces. Appliqué the head, hair, arms and bodice.
3 Cut out and appliqué the skirt separately.

Fig 1
Template
Actual size 4½in square

This is the whole block at full size. Arrows indicate the direction of fabric stripe on dress. Draw balance marks across each seam line (see Techniques: Mosaic Patchwork).

A square with small cornerstones

Original patchwork blocks: 69, 83

Block size: 4½in (11.4cm) square finished

Original method: mosaic patchwork

Modern method: machine patchwork

Original Method

1 Cut out and tack (baste) all pieces.
2 Oversew two of the border strips to opposite sides of the centre square.
3 Sew one cornerstone square to each end of two remaining border strips.
4 Sew these units to the block centre, lining up the corner squares.

Modern Method

1 Cut four 1½in (3.8cm) squares, four 1½in x 3in (3.8cm x 7.6cm) strips and one 3in (7.6cm) square.
2 Machine sew two of the border strips to opposite sides of the centre square.
3 Sew one cornerstone square to each end of two remaining border strips.
4 Sew these to the block centre, lining up the corner squares.

TIP
The centre square of the original block 69 has rotted away to reveal the recycled paper template. If you are re-creating the look of the original coverlet, try using a print with a similar script motif.

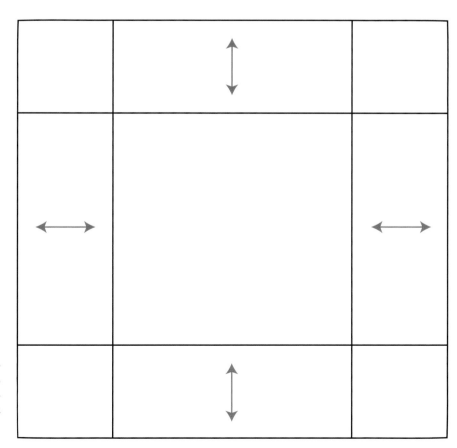

Fig 1
Template
Actual size 4½in (11.4cm) square
This is the whole block at full size. Arrows show the fabric stripe direction on original block 69. Draw balance marks across each seam line (see Techniques: Mosaic Patchwork).

An asymmetric shape

Original patchwork blocks: 70, 82 (mirror image)

Block size: 4½in (11.4cm) square finished

Original method: mosaic patchwork

Modern method: appliqué

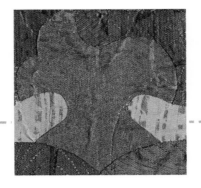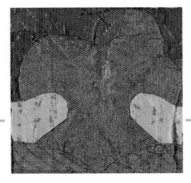

Original Method

1 Cut out and tack (baste) all pieces.
2 Oversew the two top background sections to the main motif.
3 Sew the yellow side pieces to the motif, and then sew the bottom pieces to the block to finish.

We don't know exactly what the shape in this pattern represents but it looks like some kind of billhook or agricultural blade. It most closely resembles an antique mistletoe cutter rather than a random shape and perhaps it was included because it had some special significance for the coverlet's maker.

Fig 1
Template
Actual size 4½in (11.4cm) square

This is the whole block at full size. Flip the template to make a mirror image of the design for a second block. Draw balance marks across each seam line (see Techniques: Mosaic Patchwork).

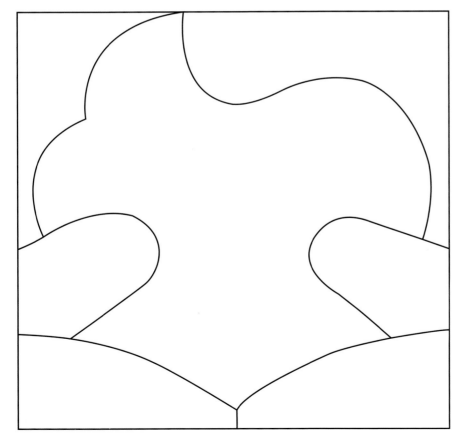

Modern Method

1 Make the block background first. Cut a 5in (12.7cm) square from the lightest background fabric and use this as the block foundation.
2 Use the top and bottom parts of the block template to cut the dark background sections with an extra ¼in (6mm) allowance all round (see Techniques: Appliqué). Line up the outside edge of these pieces with the top left and bottom right corners of the block and turn under ¼in (6mm) where they overlap the yellow side pieces. Leave raw the edges that will be under the centre appliqué. Pin and then sew in place.
3 Cut out the motif with an appropriate seam allowance and appliqué to the centre of the block, covering the raw edges of the upper corner pieces.

For a simplified block, omit the background appliqués.

Pattern 37

Pattern 37

A pheasant

Original patchwork blocks: 71, 81 (mirror image)

Block size: 4½in (11.4cm) square finished

Original method: mosaic patchwork

Modern method: appliqué

Original Method

1 Cut out and tack (baste) all pieces.

2 Oversew the beak to the top corner triangles, so it doesn't get lost.

3 Sew the diagonal line in the top left background piece. Sew this section to the top of the body.

4 Sew the diagonal line in the pieced lower background section and add the beak and background pieces. Sew this to the breast and legs. Sew the background piece under the tail.

5 Embroider the eye to finish (see Techniques: Embroidering Eyes).

Modern Method

1 Make the block background first. Cut a 5in (12.7cm) square from the lightest background fabric and use this as the block foundation. Cut the remaining background pieces with an extra ¼in (6mm) allowance all round (see Techniques: Appliqué).

2 Line up the outside edge of these pieces with the top left and bottom right corners of the block and turn under ¼in (6mm) where they overlap the background square and the next side piece, leaving the edges raw that go under the bird. Pin and sew.

3 Cut the out the body and beak, adding an appropriate seam allowance. Pin the body to the block, arranging the beak underneath, so it's overlapped by the head, and then appliqué.

For a simplified block, omit the background appliqués, or use Pattern 3 to make a diagonally quartered background.

Fig 1
Template
Actual size 4½in (11.4cm) square

This is the whole block at full size. Flip the template to make a mirror image of the design for a second block. Draw balance marks across each seam line (see Techniques: Mosaic Patchwork). The template and instructions are based on original block 81, which has an extra background piece under the beak (as shown by the dashed line) – include this if you wish.

Four triangle-squares on point

Original patchwork blocks: 72, 80, 84, 95, 149, 152

Block size: 4½in (11.4cm) square finished

Original method: mosaic patchwork

Modern method: machine patchwork

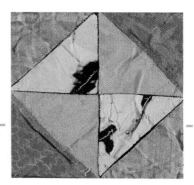

Original Method

1 Cut out and tack (baste) all pieces.
2 Oversew the triangles together into squares and then sew squares together to make the block. Match balance lines throughout the block.

Modern Method

1 Cut four 3⅛in (7.9cm) squares and then cut them in half diagonally.
2 Machine sew the triangles together into squares. Sew the squares together to make the block.

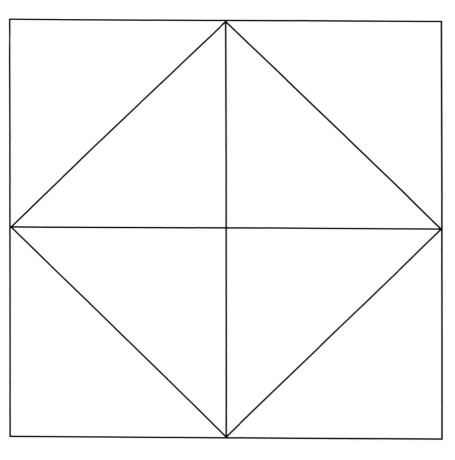

IDEA
Original blocks 72, 80, 149 and 152 all used black silk in the centre triangles, now rotted, so the value contrast when new was much greater than the blocks have today.

Fig 1
Template
Actual size 4½in (11.4cm) square
This is the whole block at full size.
Draw balance marks across each seam line
(see Techniques: Mosaic Patchwork).

A square framed by sets of triangles

Original patchwork blocks: 73, 79, 87, 92,108,113, 120, 128, 133, 143

Block size: 4½in (11.4cm) square finished

Original method: mosaic patchwork

Modern method: machine patchwork

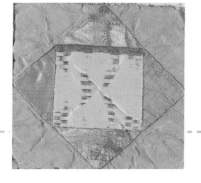

Original Method

1 Cut out and tack (baste) all pieces.
2 Oversew the inner triangles to each side of the centre square. Match balance lines throughout the block.
3 Sew the outer triangles to the block to finish.

Modern Method

1 Cut one 2¾in (7in) centre square. Cut one 3½in (8.9cm) square and quarter it diagonally for the inner triangles. Cut two 3⅛in (7.9cm) squares and cut them in half diagonally for the corners.
2 For a diagonally striped corner effect, like original blocks 87 and 92, fussy cut four triangles, using pieces from the template, from a 1¾in (4.4cm) wide strip, adding a ¼in (6mm) seam allowance all round.
3 Machine sew the inner triangles to each side of the centre square. Sew the outer triangles to the block to finish.

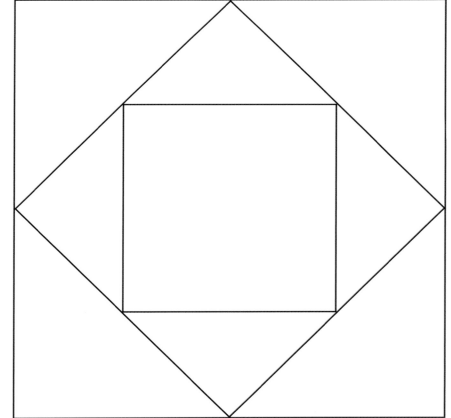

Fig 1
Template
Actual size 4½in (11.4cm) square
This is the whole block at full size.
Draw balance marks across each seam line
(see Techniques: Mosaic Patchwork).

Four tulips

Original patchwork blocks: 74, 78, 122, 126

Block size: 4½in (11.4cm) square finished

Original method: mosaic patchwork

Modern method: appliqué

The striped silk used in original block 74 was probably used to imitate the look of 'bizarres', the most expensive streaked tulips of the 'Tulip Mania' craze of the 1630s.

Original Method

1 Cut out and tack (baste) all pieces.
2 Oversew the pairs of corner pieces into the Vs of the petals and sew the corner mitres together, working from the outer corner. Match balance lines throughout the block.
3 Sew one stem piece to each larger background piece and sew the centre of the block together.
4 Insert one tulip corner section into each into each corner of the block.

Modern Method

1 Cut one 5in (12.7cm) background square. Cut two 2in x ¾in (5cm x 2cm) strips for the stems and press in half lengthwise.
2 Cut four tulips, adding an appropriate seam allowance (see Techniques: Appliqué). Lightly mark a diagonal cross in the block centre. Position and sew the first stem piece (see Techniques: Appliqué Stems), and then add the second stem.
3 Position and appliqué each tulip in turn.

Fig 1
Template
Actual size 4½in (11.4cm) square
This is the whole block at full size.
Draw balance marks across each seam line (see Techniques: Mosaic Patchwork).

A single flower

Original patchwork blocks: 75, 125

Block size: 4½in (11.4cm) square finished

Original method: mosaic patchwork

Modern method: machine patchwork and appliqué

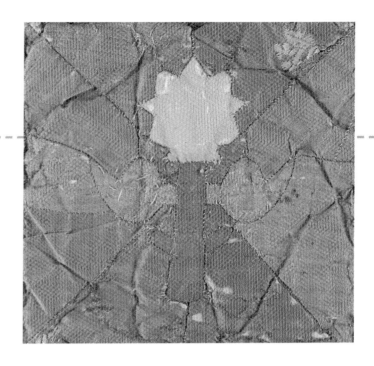

Original Method

1 Cut out and tack (baste) all pieces.
2 Oversew the two small leaf buds to the lower blue background first, so they don't get lost. Match balance lines throughout the block.
3 Sew the side pieces to either side of the lower background piece, working from the outer corner. Sew the leaves and the central background pieces immediately above them.
4 Insert the stem piece, sew the flower to the top of the stem and add the remaining background piece, completing all background seams.

Modern Method

1 Cut the pink side pieces using the templates, adding ¼in (6mm) allowance all round, and one 5in (12.7cm) blue square for the background. Fold under ¼in (6mm) on all sides of the pink pieces except the outside edges, which are lined up with the outside edge of the square, and appliqué. (Alternatively, use the instructions for Pattern 3 for a simpler background.)
2 Cut the flower, stem, leaves and leaf buds, adding an appropriate seam allowance (see Techniques: Appliqué).
3 Position and appliqué the leaf buds, and then the leaves, stem and flower.

Fig 1
Template
Actual size 4½in (11.4cm) square
This is the whole block at full size.
Draw balance marks across each seam line
(see Techniques: Mosaic Patchwork).

A single tulip

Original patchwork blocks: 76, 99, 101, 124

Block size: 4½in (11.4cm) square finished

Original method: mosaic patchwork

Modern method: machine patchwork and appliqué

Original Method

1 Cut out and tack (baste) all pieces.

2 Oversew the stem between the two lower background pieces, so it doesn't get lost. Match balance lines throughout the block.

3 Assemble the whole block background, sewing from the outer corners inwards.

4 Insert the flower into the block.

Modern Method

1 To make the background, use one of the identical triangle templates from Pattern 3 to cut two triangles from each fabric, cutting from a 2⅞in (7.3cm) wide strip and adding a ¼in (6mm) allowance to each piece. Fussy cut the pieces so the stripes line up to form a centre square if required.

2 Assemble the block, sewing the triangles together in pairs.

3 Cut one strip 1¾in x ¾in (4.4cm x 2cm) for the stem and press in half lengthwise.

4 Lightly mark a vertical line for the stem centre and then position and sew the stem (see Techniques: Appliqué Stems).

5 Cut out the tulip, adding an appropriate seam allowance and appliqué in position.

Fig 1
Template
Actual size 4½in (11.4cm) square

This is the whole block at full size. Draw balance marks across each line (see Techniques: Mosaic Patchwork).

A triple flower

Original patchwork blocks: 77, 123

Block size: 4½in (11.4cm) square finished

Original method: mosaic patchwork

Modern method: appliqué

Original Method

1 Cut out and tack (baste) all pieces.

2 Oversew the two small leaf buds to the lower shot background first, sew the gold background pieces together and insert the leaves, and then sew the flower stems to the gold background on either side.

3 Sew the upper background to the block, insert the flowers and then the centre stem piece.

4 Sew all remaining seams.

Modern Method

1 Use the templates to cut the gold background section in one piece going behind the stem. Cut the lower shot piece, adding ¼in (6mm) all round. Cut a 5in (12.7cm) beige square for the background.

2 Fold under ¼in (6mm) on the top diagonals of the gold piece, leaving edges raw behind the buds and stems, line up with the outside edge of the square and then appliqué. Fold under the diagonals on the shot piece the same way and appliqué.

3 Cut the flower, stem and leaves separately, adding seam allowance. For separate pieces, position and appliqué leaf buds, then leaves and stems, overlapping the base of leaf buds, leaves and side stems with the main stem. Appliqué the flowers to finish.

Fig 1
Template
Actual size 4½in (11.4cm) square

This is the whole block at full size. Draw balance marks across seam lines (see Techniques: Mosaic Patchwork). Block 77 has the stem and leaves made from separate pieces, but in Block 123 they are made from one piece, including the leaf buds. The template shows the additional joins.

Four small squares on point

Original patchwork blocks: 85, 86, 93, 94, 106, 107, 114, 115, 150, 151, 170, 171

Block size: 4in (10.2cm) finished

Original method: mosaic patchwork

Modern method: machine patchwork

Original Method

1 Cut out and tack (baste) all pieces.
2 Oversew the squares together in pairs and join the pairs to make the block centre.
3 Sew the corner triangles to the block centre. Match balance lines throughout the block.

Fig 1
Template
Actual size 4in (10.2cm) square

This is the whole block at full size. Note that this block is 4in (10.2cm) square, not the usual 4½in (11.4cm). For the 4½in version, see Pattern 29. Draw balance marks across each seam line (see Techniques: Mosaic Patchwork).

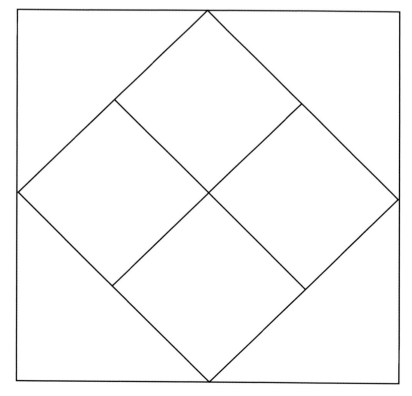

Modern Method

1 Cut four 2in (5cm) squares for the centre – it is easier to cut these a little oversized and trim the four-patch centre later, or use the template to cut these, adding ¼in (6mm) all round. Cut two 2⅞in (7.3cm) squares in half diagonally for corner triangles.
2 Sew the squares together in pairs and join the pairs to make the block centre.
3 Sew the corner triangles to the block centre. Trim the four-patch block centre to 3⁵⁄₁₆in (8.4cm) before adding the corner triangles.

IDEA

These smaller 4in (10.2cm) blocks are used only to fill the corners of Pattern 48, but could be used in their own right with narrow borders or sashing between the blocks.

Pattern 45

A curled flower

Original patchwork blocks: 88, 112

Block size: 4½in (11.4cm) square finished

Original method: mosaic patchwork

Modern method: appliqué

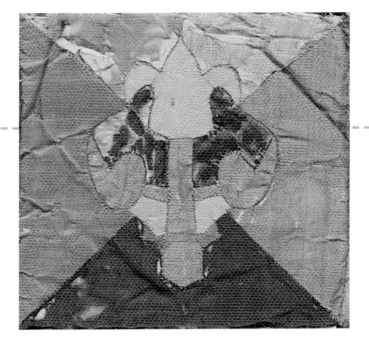

Original Method

1 Cut out and tack (baste) all pieces.

2 Oversew the leaf buds to the lower background piece, so they don't get lost.

3 Sew the background side pieces to the lower background piece, from the block corners.

4 Sew the side stems to above the small, pale background pieces and below the brown central background pieces, then sew these to the block. Insert the leaves and the main stem into the block and sew the central part of the flower to the block.

5 Sew the curled petals to the upper background piece and sew to the block.

Modern Method

1 Cut a 5in (12.7cm) gold square for the background.

2 Use the templates to cut the lower background piece, adding ¼in (6mm) all round. Fold under ¼in (6mm) on the top diagonals, leaving edges raw behind leaf buds and stem. Line up with the outside edge of the square and appliqué. Add the upper light background section the same way.

3 Add the darker central background fabric and light section above the leaf buds the same way, cutting each as one piece, so fabric continues under the stem.

4 Cut and appliqué the flower, stem and leaves, overlapping them appropriately.

Fig 1
Template
Actual size 4½in (11.4cm) square

This is the whole block at full size. Draw balance marks across each seam line (see Techniques: Mosaic Patchwork). Dashed lines show optional seams. The template is drawn from original block 112.

A small eight-point star

Original patchwork blocks: 89, 90, 110, 111

Block size: 4½in (11.4cm) square finished

Original method: mosaic patchwork

Modern method: machine patchwork

Original Method

1 Cut out and tack (baste) all pieces. Note: the thin diamonds that make the star are not symmetrical, as the block has been drafted on a nine-patch square grid, not the way most eight-point stars are drafted today. Put an identification mark and direction arrow on the back of your diamond templates so you can see which end points to the centre and the correct position for each diamond.
2 Follow steps 2 and 3 of Pattern 49 Original Method to sew the block.

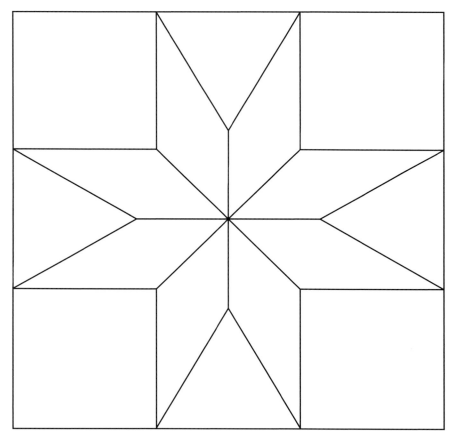

Modern Method

1 See note above regarding non-symmetrical diamonds.
2 Follow steps 1–3 of Pattern 49 Modern Method to sew the block, cutting four 2in (5cm) squares for the corners and using the templates to cut the other pieces.

Fig 1
Template
Actual size 4½in (11.4cm) square

This is the whole block at full size. Draw balance marks across each seam line (see Techniques: Mosaic Patchwork). This is a smaller version of original Block 100, used to fill the corners of the larger block. Block 100 is drafted on a nine-patch arrangement, so the block was divided into thirds vertically and horizontally. This block is the regular 4½in (11.4cm) size, rather than the smaller 4in (10.2cm) square Pattern 44, which forms the corners of Pattern 48.

A wavy flower

Original patchwork blocks: 91, 109

Block size: 4½in (11.4cm) square finished

Original method: mosaic patchwork

Modern method: appliqué

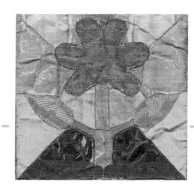

Original Method

1 Cut out and tack (baste) all pieces.

2 Oversew the leaf stems to the brown lower background pieces.

3 Sew the lower side pieces to the base pieces along the diagonal seams and add the leaves. Sew the yellow centre background pieces to the patchwork. Sew the main stem between these two pieces.

4 Sew the upper half of the background together in sequence and add the two top petals, then the rest of the flower.

5 Sew the two halves of the block together.

Modern Method

1 Cut one 5in (12.7cm) pink square for the background. Use the templates to cut the other background pieces, adding ¼in (6mm) allowance all round. Cut the lower brown background piece in one and add only ⅛in (3mm) allowance where it goes behind the leaf stems. Fold under ¼in (6mm) on the sides of this piece, leaving the edges raw behind the leaf stems, line up with the outside edge of the square and appliqué.

2 Starting with the centre top background piece and working outwards, add all the upper background pieces in sequence, turning under ¼in (6mm) to overlap the previous piece by a ¼in (6mm) each time. Alternatively, use Pattern 3 instructions for a simplified background.

3 Cut the flowers (in one piece), the leaves and stem, adding an appropriate seam allowance (see Techniques: Appliqué). Cut two 1¼in x ⅝in (3.2cm x 1.5cm) pieces for the leaf stems, press in half lengthwise and appliqué (see Techniques: Appliqué Stems).

4 Appliqué the leaves, main stem and flower to finish.

Fig 1
Template
Actual size 4½in (11.4cm) square

This is the whole block at full size. Draw balance marks across each seam line (see Techniques: Mosaic Patchwork). Both blocks are on their sides in the coverlet, as they surround the central star. Dashed lines show extra seams in original block 109.

A lollipop hearts star

Original patchwork blocks: 97, 103 and 161

Block size: 13½in (34.3cm) square finished

Original method: mosaic patchwork

Modern method: machine patchwork and appliqué

Block extras: Pattern 44 as a corner infill

Original Method

1 Make the eight diamond-shaped lollipop heart sections individually first. Oversew the 'sticks' between each pair of hearts to the relevant background pieces, then sew the heart to each end of the section, following the tips on piecing sharp points in Techniques: Adapting Mosaic Patchwork. Arrange these diamond pieces to form the star shape, matching up balance marks as you go.
2 Sew the two triangles to the square for each setting triangle and sew these to the relevant diamond pieces, completing four sections. For accuracy, sew longer sections from opposite ends, and finish in the centre of each section with a few stitches overlapping.
3 Sew the sections together in pairs and sew the two halves of the block together.
4 Add four square corner sections, made following Pattern 44.

Modern Method

1 Making a diamond-shaped background piece as an appliqué foundation for each lollipop hearts pair makes the block easier to construct. It is even easier to cut out these diamonds from sets of machine pieced strips rather than try to sew skinny pointed pieces together by machine.
2 Cut one 8½in x 1¾in (21.6cm x 4.4cm) strip for each side plus one 8½in x 1⅛in (21.6cm x 2.8cm) strip for the central 'lollipop stick' for all eight diamonds. Machine sew one wide strip to either side of the narrow strip and press seam allowances towards the strip. Make a template for one diamond section and use this to trim each set of strips to a diamond shape, remembering to add on a ¼in (6mm) seam allowance all round. Alternatively, fussy cut the diamonds from striped fabric, so a stripe plays the part of the lollipop 'stick'.

Fig 1
Whole block (25% size) – enlarge by 400%

Fig 1 shows the whole block reduced in scale and Fig 2 shows the upper quarter of the template at full size. A single segment is shown shaded. Follow the instructions with the Fig 2 template. The templates for the corners are not included here – see Pattern 44 for these.

3 Cut sixteen hearts from four different fabrics, adding ¼in (6mm) seam allowance at the sides of the diamonds and the appropriate turning allowance for your appliqué technique across the curves at the top of each heart (see Techniques: Appliqué). Appliqué a heart to each end of each diamond block and trim excess fabric from the back. Stay stitching around the diamond – machine sewing ⅛in (3mm) away from the edge before the diamond is cut out – will stabilize the bias-cut edges and stop them stretching while you appliqué the hearts to each end.

4 Make the four setting triangle sections from one 2⅞in (7.3cm) square, cut in half diagonally to make two right-angled triangles, and sew to one 2½in (6.4cm) square.
5 Machine sew the lollipop hearts diamonds together in pairs and, following the information on inset seams (Techniques: Machine Piecing Mitres), insert the setting triangle sections.
6 Sew the four sections together to make the centre of this block and add four of Pattern 44 to complete the corners.

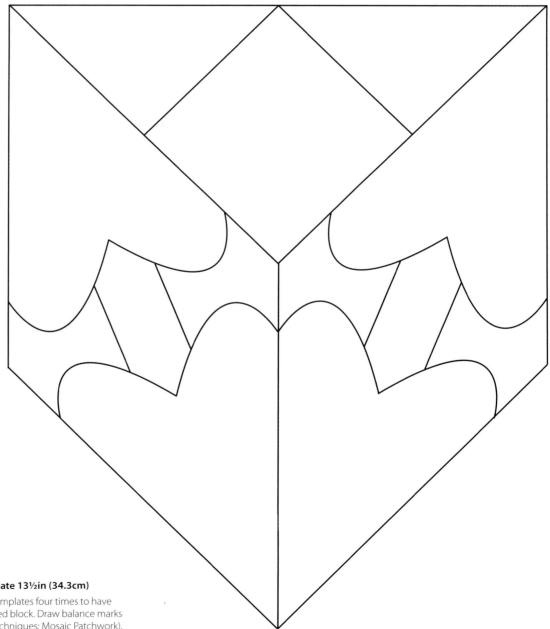

Fig 2
Template (quarter)
Actual size of whole template 13½in (34.3cm)
Trace and cut out the Fig 2 templates four times to have enough for one mosaic-pieced block. Draw balance marks across each seam line (see Techniques: Mosaic Patchwork).

An eight-pointed star

Original patchwork block: 100

Block size: 13½in (34.3cm) square finished

Original method: mosaic patchwork

Modern method: machine patchwork

Block extras: Pattern 46 as a corner infill

Original Method

1 Note – the thin diamonds that make the star are not symmetrical, as the block has been drafted on a nine-patch square grid, not the way most eight-point stars are drafted today. The red diamond will always be the right-hand point and the ivory floral the left-hand point. Make sure you mark the back of your templates so you know which diamond is which.
2 Arrange the diamond pieces to form the star shape and oversew together in pairs. Add the blue triangles at the edge. For accuracy, sew longer sections from opposite ends, matching up balance marks as you go and finishing in the centre of each section with a few stitches overlapping.
3 Sew the star sections together in pairs and then sew the two halves of the block together. Add four square corner sections following the pattern for Pattern 46.

Modern Method

1 See note above regarding non-symmetrical diamonds. Use one of the diamond templates to cut four ivory fabric diamonds and flip it over to cut four red diamonds, so they are mirror images of the ivory diamonds, adding a ¼in (6mm) seam allowance all round as you go.
2 Cut out four blue triangles, adding a ¼in (6mm) all round. Machine sew the diamonds together in pairs and, following the information on inset seams (Techniques: Machine Piecing Mitres), insert the setting triangle sections.
3 Sew the four sections together to make the centre of this block and add four of Pattern 46 to complete the corners.

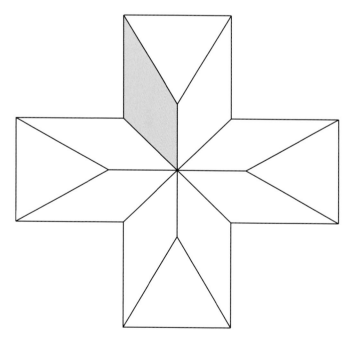

Fig 1
Whole block (25% size) – enlarge by 400%

Fig 1 shows the whole block reduced in scale and Fig 2 shows the upper quarter of the template at full size. The templates for the corners, Pattern 46, are not included here (see Pattern 46 for these). Follow the instructions with the template.

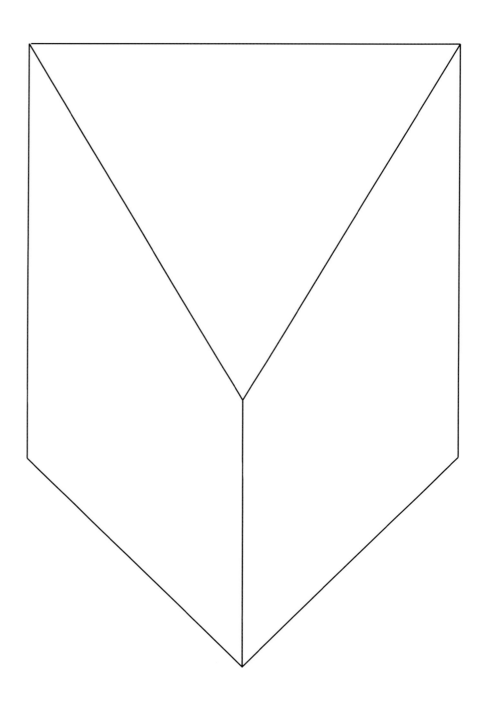

IDEA

The block may include one of the coverlet maker's most precious fabrics, prominently displayed in the centre of the patchwork – a silk with a painted or printed design of stylized flowers and foliage on an ivory background. A hand-painted reproduction was made for the replica coverlet. You could combine masked and hand-painted strips with block printing to make a similar pattern, or look for a commercially printed cotton with a suitable design.

Fig 2
Template (quarter)
Actual size of whole template 13½in (34.3cm)

Trace and cut out the Fig 2 templates four times to have enough for one block. Draw balance marks across each seam line (see Techniques: Mosaic Patchwork).

Carved double fleur-de-lys

Original patchwork blocks: 117, 131

Block size: 9in x 4½in (22.9cm x 11.4cm)

Original method: mosaic patchwork

Modern method: appliqué (optional patchwork)

Original Method

1 Cut out and tack (baste) all pieces.
2 Start by sewing the cream inner background sections to the inside of the brown curved pieces. Match balance lines throughout the block.
3 Sew the cream side pieces to the top and bottom striped pieces respectively, and sew these to the outside of the brown curved pieces.
4 Sew the gold background pieces to join the top and bottom of the block.
5 Join the centre brown pieces through the block centre and insert into the block to finish.

Modern Method

1 Cut one 9½in x 5in (24.1cm x 12.7cm) cream piece for the background and cut two gold side pieces using the templates, adding ¼in (6mm) allowance all round. Fold under a ¼in (6mm) at the top and bottom of each gold piece, line up the outer edges and appliqué to the centre of the background piece. Alternatively, piece the block background from three strips – two 3⅞in x 5in (9.8cm x 12.7cm) cream strips and one 2¾in x 5in (7cm x 12.7cm) gold strip.
2 Use the template to cut two pieces of red stripe with an extra ¼in (6mm) allowance all round (see Techniques: Appliqué). Line up the outside edge of these pieces with the top and bottom of the block and turn under ¼in (6mm) along the diagonals, leaving the edges raw that will be overlapped by the fleur-de-lys. Pin and sew.
3 Cut out the fleur-de-lys in four pieces, with an appropriate seam allowance all round. Appliqué to the centre of the block, sewing the curved end pieces first and covering the raw edges of the background pieces. Seam the centre pieces together and then appliqué the finished double fleur, covering the raw edges of the previous pieces.

For a simpler appliqué shape, cut the double fleurs in one piece, although appliquéing the deep V-shaped indents will be necessary.

Pattern 50 features another very effective design that is similar to a fleur-de-lys, but where the exact origin of the motif is unknown.

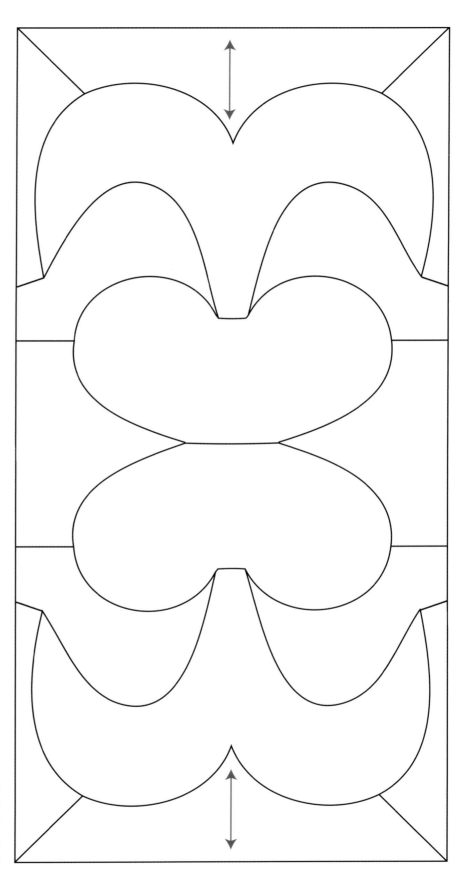

Fig 1
Template
Actual size 9in x 4½in (22.9cm x 11.4cm)
This is the whole block at full size. The
arrows indicate the fabric stripe direction.
Draw balance marks across each seam line
(see Techniques: Mosaic Patchwork).

A fleur-de-lys variation

Original patchwork blocks: 118, 130

Block size: 4½in (11.4cm) square finished

Original method: mosaic patchwork

Modern method: appliqué

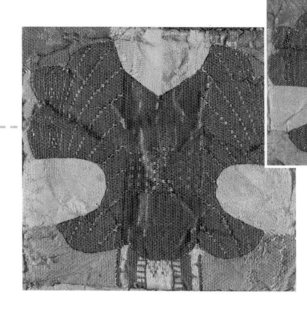

Original Method

1 Cut out and tack (baste) all pieces.
2 Start by sewing the V section to the top of the fleur-de-lys. Match balance lines throughout the block.
3 Sew the lower background pieces together and sew to the fleur-de-lys.
4 Sew the side pieces to the fleur-de-lys and add the top corners to finish.

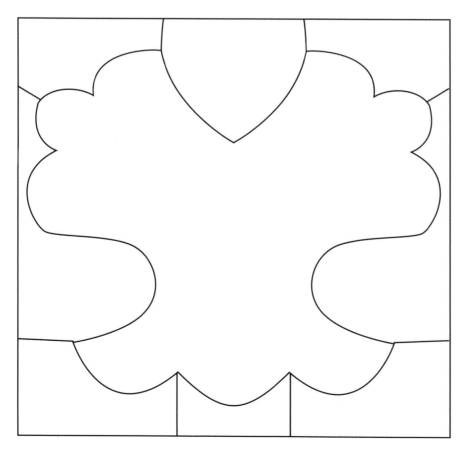

Modern Method

1 Cut one 5in (12.7cm) square in light fabric for the background. Use the template to cut out the other background pieces with an extra ¼in (6mm) allowance all round (see Techniques: Appliqué). Line up the outside edge of these pieces with the block corners. Turn under a ¼in (6mm) where the upper corner piece edges line up with the fleur-de-lys edges, leaving the edges that will be overlapped by the fleur-de-lys raw. Pin and sew.
2 Appliqué the lower background pieces in the same way, finishing with the bottom centre stripe.
3 Cut out the fleur-de-lys with an appropriate seam allowance and appliqué to the centre of the block, covering the raw edges of the corner pieces.
   For a simplified block, omit the background appliqués.

Fig 1
Template
Actual size 4½in (11.4cm) square

This is the whole block at full size.
Draw balance marks across each seam line
(see Techniques: Mosaic Patchwork).

A deer

Original patchwork blocks: 119 and 129 mirror image

Block size: 4½in (11.4cm) square finished

Original method: mosaic patchwork

Modern method: appliqué

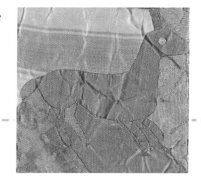
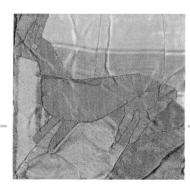

Original Method

1 Assemble the block in sections. Match the balance lines throughout the block. Sew the smallest pieces first, so they don't get lost.

2 Oversew the antlers to the green striped top piece, following the tips on piecing sharp points (Techniques: Adapting Mosaic Patchwork).

3 Sew the two inner legs to the gold lower background section. Sew the other two legs to the blue piece and the striped piece respectively, and sew these to either side of the lower gold section. Sew the tail to the upper striped section.

4 Sew the upper and lower sections to the body to finish the block.

Modern Method

1 Make the block background following the method given for Pattern 37 (see also Techniques: Appliqué onto Foundation Squares).

2 Cut all the pieces for the deer's body. Add the appropriate turning allowance for your chosen appliqué technique (see Techniques: Appliqué). Position and appliqué the legs and antlers, and then the body.

For a simplified appliqué-only block, replace the pieced background with a 5in (12.7cm) square and cut the deer as one piece.

Fig 1
Template
Actual size 4½in (11.4cm) square

This shows the whole block. Flip the template to make a mirror image of the design for a second block. Draw balance marks across each seam line (see Techniques: Mosaic Patchwork). Moving the legs slightly further apart (with more space between the two back legs and front legs), may make this block easier to sew.

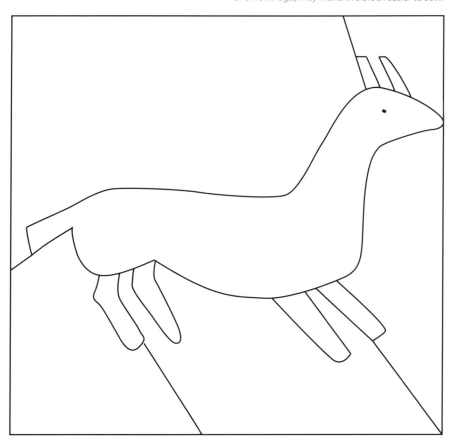

A cockerel

Original patchwork blocks: 134, 142 (mirror image)

Block size: 4½in (11.4cm) square finished

Original method: mosaic patchwork

Modern method: appliqué

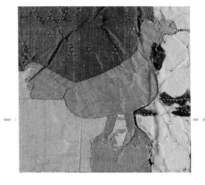
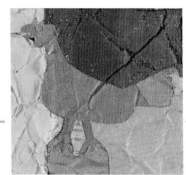

Original Method

1 Cut out and tack (baste) all pieces.

2 Start by sewing the piece between the bird's legs, joining the legs together, and sew to the gold background piece. Match balance lines throughout the block. Sew the lower background pieces to either side of this.

3 Sew the open beak infill to the head.

4 Sew the small top corner piece to the upper striped background section and then sew to the top of the bird. Sew to the bottom half of the block. Embroider the eye to finish (see Techniques: Embroidering Eyes).

Modern Method

1 Cut one 5in (12.7cm) square in light fabric for the background. Use the template to cut the other background pieces with an extra ¼in (6mm) allowance all round (see Techniques: Appliqué). Cut the background in front of the bird in one piece (this was black silk originally).

2 Line up this background piece and pin to the background. Turn under a ¼in (6mm) where the black and the blue and brown striped background pieces overlap this, leaving the edges that will be under the body raw. Line up the edge of these pieces with their respective block corners and appliqué. Appliqué the piece between the legs.

3 Turn under ¼in (6mm) on either side of the gold background piece and appliqué to the background.

4 Appliqué the legs and then the rest of the body. Embroider the eye to finish.

Fig 1
Template
Actual size 4½in (11.4cm) square

This is the whole block at full size. Draw balance marks across each seam line (see Techniques: Mosaic Patchwork).

A lion rampant

Original patchwork block: 137

Block size: 4½in (11.4cm) square finished

Original method: mosaic patchwork

Modern method: appliqué

Original Method

1 Cut out and tack (baste) all pieces.

2 Start by oversewing all the background pieces together, apart from the striped piece behind the lion's back and the lower gold corner. Match balance lines throughout the block.

3 Sew the head and the underside of the body to the background patchwork, right round to the tip of the tail.

4 Sew the striped background section to the lion's back and finish with the gold corner section that just touches the tip of his tail.

Modern Method

1 Cut one 5in (12.7cm) square in light blue for the background. Use the template to cut the other background pieces, adding an extra ¼in (6mm) all round (see Techniques: Appliqué). Line up the striped background piece and pin to the background.

2 Turn under ¼in (6mm) where the gold background corner pieces overlap this and the background square, leaving edges raw that will be under the body. Line up the edge of these pieces with their respective block corners and appliqué.

3 Turn under ¼in (6mm) on the diagonal edges of the brown background piece and appliqué to the background.

4 Position the lion to cover all the raw edges and appliqué in place to finish.

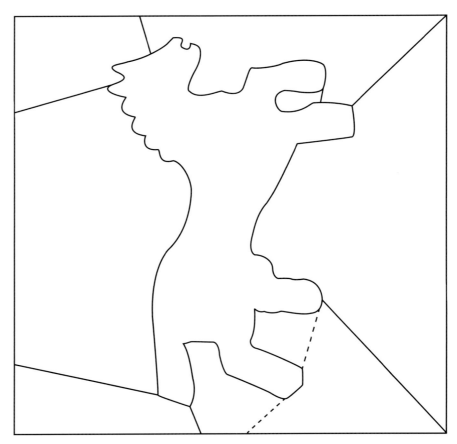

Fig 1
Template
Actual size 4½in (11.4cm) square

This is the whole block at full size. Draw balance marks across each seam line (see Techniques: Mosaic Patchwork). The dashed lines are optional mosaic piecing lines used for the replica coverlet.

An enclosed square on point

Original patchwork block: 138

Block size: 4½in (11.4cm) square finished

Original method: mosaic patchwork

Modern method: machine patchwork

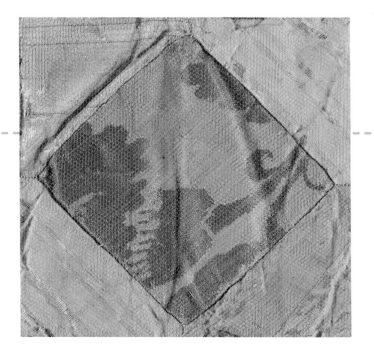

Original Method

1 Cut out and tack (baste) all pieces.
2 Oversew the corner pieces to the centre square in sequence. Match balance lines throughout the block.
3 Sew the short side seams to finish the block, working from the outside edge inwards.

Modern Method

1 Cut one 3⁵⁄₁₆in (8.4cm) square for the centre.
2 Cut the four corner pieces from the templates and add on ¼in (6mm) seam allowance all round. Sew the corner pieces to the centre square.
3 Finish the block by sewing the short side seams (see Techniques: Machine Piecing Mitres).

Fig 1
Template
Actual size 4½in (11.4cm) square

This is the whole block at full size. Draw balance marks across each seam line (see Techniques: Mosaic Patchwork). This block is similar to Pattern 30 but is not exactly the same, as the central square on point is smaller and the corner pieces are not triangles but pentagons, with very short vertical and horizontal seams where they meet.

A unicorn

Original patchwork block: 139

Block size: 4½in (11.4cm) square finished

Original method: mosaic patchwork

Modern method: appliqué

Original Method

1 Cut out and tack (baste) all pieces.

2 Oversew the horn to the upper striped piece. Sew to the blue damask.

3 Sew the tail pieces together and add to the lower edge of the blue damask. Sew the striped background piece to this.

4 Sew the brown silk piece to the upper light blue background. Sew the light blue lower background pieces together and sew the separate hind leg to this.

5 Sew the head to the body. Sew the head/body to the right-hand half of the block. Sew the remaining background sections to the body. Finish with the diagonal seams on the left of the block, sewing from the corners inwards.

Modern Method

1 Cut one 5in (12.7cm) square in light blue fabric as background. Use the template to cut the other background pieces with an extra ¼in (6mm) allowance all round (see Techniques: Appliqué).

2 Make the background following the method given for Pattern 37.

3 Cut out the unicorn, either in one piece or adapting the pattern, keeping the hind leg, horn and tail as separate pieces to avoid tight Vs. Position the unicorn to cover all raw edges, and appliqué. If in more than one piece, make sure the body overlaps the top of the leg, the tail base and horn base.

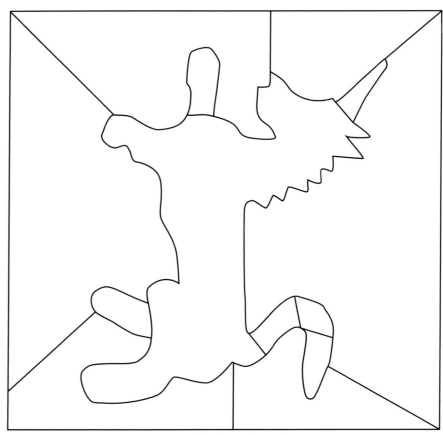

Fig 1
Template
Actual size 4½in (11.4cm) square
This is the whole block at full size. Draw balance marks across each seam line (see Techniques: Mosaic Patchwork).

A swag with trefoil

Original patchwork blocks: 145 and 156

Block size: 9in (22.9cm) square finished

Original method: mosaic patchwork

Modern method: appliqué

Original Method

1 Assemble the block in sections. Match balance lines throughout the block. Oversew the upper background sections first. For accuracy, sew longer sections from opposite ends, matching up balance marks as you go and finishing in the centre of each oversewn seam with a few stitches overlapping.

2 Sew the lower half of the swag to the lower half of the background.

3 Sew the two halves of the block together, joining the top edge of the swag to the upper background, starting the sewing of the curves at the inner points and easing the curves together.

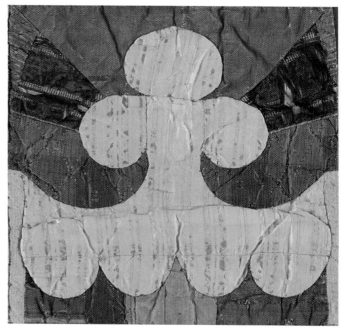

Fig 1

Whole block (25% size) – enlarge by 400%

Fig 1 shows the whole block reduced in scale and Fig 2 shows one half of the template at full size. Follow the instructions with the Fig 2 template. Fig 1 shows the additional seam lines (shown as dashed lines) on the trefoil from original block 156.

Pattern 57 occurs twice within the coverlet (original blocks 145 and 156). The different fabrics used are shown in these two pictures, so refer to them if you are re-creating the look of the original coverlet.

Modern Method

1 Cut one 9½in (23.1cm) background square from the centre top background fabric. Use the template to cut the other background pieces with an extra ¼in (6mm) allowance all round (see Techniques: Appliqué onto Foundation Squares).

2 Turn under ¼in (6mm) along the top diagonal edge of the upper background pieces, pin and appliqué. Repeat with the next set of background pieces and the bottom background pieces, finishing with the blue piece at the bottom centre. Leave the edges raw under the trefoil and swag.

3 Cut out and appliqué the trefoil, adding an appropriate turning allowance for your chosen appliqué technique (see Techniques: Appliqué).

For a simplified appliqué-only block, replace the pieced background with a 9½in (24.1cm) square.

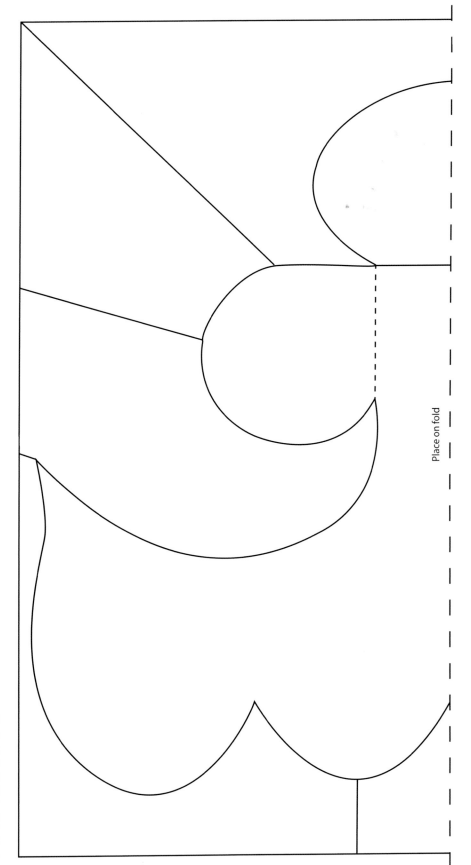

Place on fold

Fig 2
Template (half)
Actual size of whole template
9in (22.9m) square

Fold a 9in (22.9cm) paper square in half and trace off the template, lining up the long dashed line with the fabric fold. Repeat the design for the other half by tracing or carefully cut out the pattern through all the layers with the paper still folded. Draw balance marks across each seam line (see Techniques: Mosaic Patchwork).

A cat with a fish

Original patchwork blocks: 146, 155 (mirror image)

Block size: 4½in (11.4cm) square finished

Original method: mosaic patchwork

Modern method: appliqué

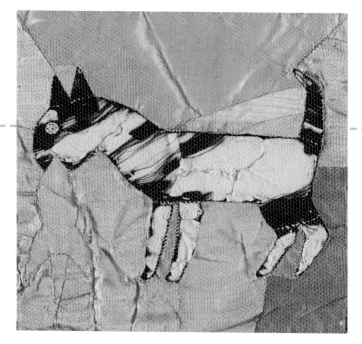

Original Method

1 Cut out and tack (baste) all pieces. Oversew the smaller pieces first. Sew the forward ear to the light blue background corner, then sew the tiny cream background piece to the second ear. Sew these and the tail to the upper background piece. Sew the body to the upper background, from under the tail to the front of the ears.

2 Make the lower half of the block as follows. Sew the hind legs to either side of the very narrow brown background piece and sew to the lower brown background piece, leaving the rear hind leg unsewn above the bend. Sew the seam to join the hind legs to the body.

3 Sew the upper left light blue corner piece to the brown lower corner piece. Sew to the back of the body from the tip of the tail to the heel.

4 Sew the right front leg to the thin gold piece between the legs and then sew this to the large gold background piece under the neck and chin. Sew the other front leg to the gold background piece that goes under the belly and then join to the right front leg.

5 Sew the thin fish tail section to the adjacent gold background pieces. Sew to the fish.

6 Join the gold background pieces together, sew to the cat and complete the background. Embroider the eye to finish (see Techniques: Embroidering Eyes).

TIP

You can see by the pictures here that original block 146 (lower picture) has an extra horizontal seam between the fish tail and its body, which may be added if you wish.

Modern Method

1 Cut a 5in (12.7cm) square in cream for background. Use the template to cut the other background pieces with an extra ¼in (6mm) allowance all round. Cut gold background pieces as one piece. Appliqué these to the background in sequence, turning under ¼in (6mm) allowance where each piece overlaps the previous one, but leaving allowances under the body raw (see Techniques: Appliqué onto Foundation Squares).

2 Cut out the body, with the legs separate for easier appliqué, adding an appropriate seam allowance for the appliqué technique you are using.

3 Cut out the fish in one piece, pin it into position and then appliqué it.

4 Pin the body to the block and position the legs. Appliqué the legs, then the body, covering the raw edges at the top of the legs. Embroider the eye to finish (see Techniques: Embroidering Eyes).

You could simplify the making of this block by using a single 5in (12.7cm) square as background.

IDEA
The cat was originally made using black silk, which has rotted over time, but you can use any colour you wish.

Fig 1
Template
Actual size 4½in (11.4cm) square
This is the whole block at full size.
Draw balance marks across each seam line
(see Techniques: Mosaic Patchwork).

Double-framed diagonal quarters

Original patchwork block: 148, 153

Block size: 4½in (11.4cm) square finished

Original method: mosaic patchwork

Modern method: machine patchwork

Original Method

1 Cut out and tack (baste) all pieces.

2 Oversew the central triangles together in pairs and then sew them together to make the central square. Match balance lines throughout the block.

3 Sew the next set of triangles to the square. Sew on the corner triangles to finish.

Fig 1

Template

Actual size 4½in (11.4cm) square

This is the whole block at full size. Draw balance marks across each seam line (see Techniques: Mosaic Patchwork). Construct the block from the centre outwards.

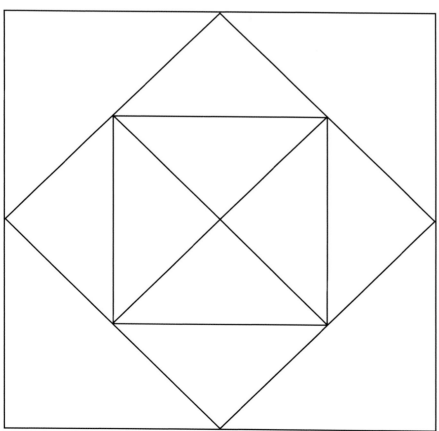

Modern Method

1 For the striped centre fabrics, either cut two 3½in (8.9cm) squares quartered diagonally (for two sets of stripes, one running parallel to the square edge and the other at right angles) or cut four triangles, two from each stripe fabric, from 1¾in (4.4cm) strips. For non-directional patterns or plains, cut two 2¾in (7cm) squares halved diagonally.

2 Cut one 3½in (8.9cm) square quartered diagonally for the next set of triangles and four 3⅛in (7.9cm) squares halved diagonally for the corner triangles.

3 Sew the central triangles together in pairs and then sew them together to make the central square.

4 Sew the next set of triangles to the patchwork square, and then sew on the corner triangles to complete the block.

Pattern 60 A lioness

Original patchwork blocks: 158, 164 (mirror image)

Block size: 4½in (11.4cm) square finished

Original method: mosaic patchwork

Modern method: appliqué

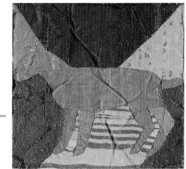

Original Method

1 Cut out and tack (baste) all pieces. Oversew all the upper background pieces together.

2 Sew the tail to the top of the lower side background piece and the rear hind leg to the side of that piece. Sew the striped narrow background piece to the left of the other hind leg. Sew the front legs to either side of the other striped narrow background piece. Sew back and front leg sections to either side of the main striped lower background piece. Sew the lower right background piece to the front leg and complete the seam to the block edge.

3 Sew the head to the body and sew the body to the lower half of the patchwork block, from the seam at the top of the hind legs to tip of nose. Sew the lioness to the top of the block, from tip of tail to tip of nose. Sew the remaining short seam to attach the tail section to the rump. Embroider the eye (see Techniques: Embroidering Eyes).

Modern Method

1 Cut one 5in (12.7cm) square for the background, to show as the striped lower background. Use the template to cut the other background pieces with an extra ¼in (6mm) allowance all round (see Techniques: Appliqué).

2 Make the background following the method given for Pattern 37.

3 Cut out all lioness pieces (head and body in one piece). Pin in place, align and appliqué the tail and legs. The tail may be cut in one with the body.

4 Appliqué the body, covering the raw edges of the background pieces and the raw ends of the legs and tail. Embroider the eye to finish.

Fig 1
Template
Actual size 4½in (11.4cm) square
This is the whole block at full size. Draw balance marks across each seam line (see Techniques: Mosaic Patchwork).

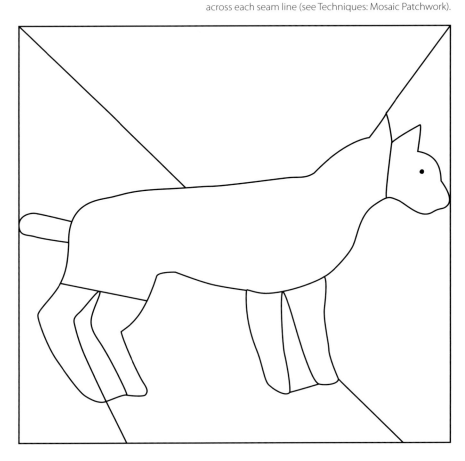

A rabbit

Original patchwork blocks: 159, 163 (mirror image)

Block size: 4½in (11.4cm) square finished

Original method: mosaic patchwork

Modern method: appliqué

Original Method

1 Cut out and tack (baste) all pieces. Start by oversewing the tail to the brown background piece and the front leg to the green background piece. Sew the tail section to the other two brown background pieces.
2 Sew the legs to either side of the small blue background piece and sew this to the larger blue piece.
3 Sew the diagonal seam to join the blue and brown background pieces and sew the brown piece to the back of the back leg.
4 Sew the small green triangle between the ears. Sew this to the remaining green background pieces, adding the centre side piece, then the lower piece, and then the top piece.
5 Sew along the lower diagonal background seam line and from the tip of the front leg, around the face to the back of the head.
6 Sew the yellow striped piece to the top of the block, sewing the diagonal seams first. Sew the remainder of the body to the background, from behind the ears, along the back to the tail. Embroider the eye to finish (see Techniques: Embroidering Eyes).

TIP
The rabbit's open mouth on both original blocks was simplified for the replica coverlet. Fig 1 shows the replica template with the mouth closed.

Modern Method

1 Cut one 5in (12.7cm) pale blue square for the background. Use the template to cut the other background pieces with an extra ¼in (6mm) allowance all round.

2 Line up the yellow striped background piece with the block edge and pin in place. Fold under ¼in (6mm) seam allowance on the diagonal edges of the brown and green background pieces, line up and appliqué (see Techniques: Appliqué). Leave raw all edges that will be under the body.

3 Cut out all the rabbit pieces with turning allowances. Pin the pieces in place and align and appliqué the tail, legs and ears.

4 Sew down the body, which may be cut in one piece. Appliqué the body, covering the raw edges of the background pieces and the raw ends of the tail, legs and ears. Embroider the eye to finish (see Techniques: Embroidering Eyes).

Simplify the pattern by replacing the appliqué background with Pattern 3.

IDEA

In the original coverlet the rabbit was made in black silk. This has rotted over time due to the iron filings used to fix the black dye. You can make the rabbit any colour you like.

Fig 1
Template
Actual size 4½in (11.4cm) square
This is the whole block at full size. Draw balance marks across each seam line (see Techniques: Mosaic Patchwork). The template shows original block 163 mirrored, as the piecing is a little more logical. Flip the template to make the second block.

Pattern 62 · A swan

Original patchwork blocks: 160, 162 (mirror image)

Block size: 4½in (11.4cm) square finished

Original method: mosaic patchwork

Modern method: appliqué

Original Method

1 Cut out and tack (baste) all pieces.

2 Sew the two toes on the foot to the small pink triangles and then sew these to the background pieces on either side. Sew the main part of the leg to join these background sections.

3 Make the body as follows. Sew the wings to either side of the tail piece and sew this section to the body. Sew the beak to the head.

4 Sew the upper background pieces together in sequence, including the small gold piece next to the beak.

5 Now sew the upper background to the lower background section.

6 Sew the swan into the block, from the tip of the tail to the beak's point, along the back and underside of the body. Embroider the eye to finish (see Techniques: Embroidering Eyes).

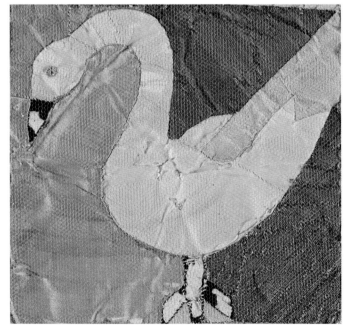

IDEA
The swan was simplified for the replica coverlet, with the body, wing and tail cut all in one piece, so you could use this quicker method if you prefer. Fig 1 shows the pieces used in the original coverlet.

Modern Method

1 Cut one 5in (12.7cm) square in gold fabric for the background.

2 Use the template to cut the other background pieces with an extra ¼in (6mm) allowance all round (see Techniques: Appliqué).

3 Line up each blue/brown background piece and pin to the background. Turn under ¼in (6mm) where the pink upper corner pieces overlap the upper blue/brown piece and the background square, leaving the edges that will be under the body raw. Line up the edge of these pieces with the block corner and appliqué.

4 Cut out the tail, body, small wing, beak and leg, plus the pink triangles for under the foot, with appropriate seam allowances. The pink triangles can be cut as one piece. The leg may be cut in one piece.

5 Pin the main part of the body in place. Line up and appliqué the small wing, beak and leg, adding small pink triangles under the foot. Leave the edge of the small wing raw on the body side and overlap and appliqué the tail, leaving the edge on the body side raw.

6 Position the body to cover all raw edges and appliqué.

7 Embroider the eye to finish the block (see Techniques: Embroidering Eyes).

TIP
The swan's foot and leg could be cut in one piece, without the small pink triangles, to look more like a webbed foot. It would also be easier to sew this way.

Fig 1
Template
Actual size 4½in (11.4cm) square
This is the whole block at full size.
Draw balance marks across each seam line
(see Techniques: Mosaic Patchwork).

<table>
<tr><td>Pattern 63</td><td></td></tr>
</table>

A quatrefoil fleur-de-lys with triangles centre

Original patchwork blocks: 166, 175

Block size: 13½in (34.3cm)

Original method: mosaic patchwork

Modern method: machine patchwork and appliqué

Original Method

1 Cut out and tack (baste) all pieces.
2 Make the quatrefoil fleur-de-lys. Oversew each fleur section to the relevant centre triangle. Match balance lines throughout the block.
3 Sew the fleur units together in pairs along the centre seams and then sew the pairs together to complete the quatrefoil fleur-de-lys.
4 Sew each flattened gold oval to the patchwork.
5 Sew a pink border piece to each side of the block. Finish the block by sewing the mitres, starting at the block corners.

Modern Method

1 Cut one 14in (35.6cm) square for the block background. Cut one grey and one gold 3¼in (8.3cm) square. Cut both squares in half diagonally.
2 Use the template to cut out the four fleurs-de-lys and four flattened gold ovals, with an appropriate seam allowance all round but adding a ¼in (6mm) seam allowance to the straight-line diagonal base of each fleur. Refer to Techniques: Appliqué for a choice of appliqué techniques, including needle-turn appliqué and freezer paper appliqué.
3 Machine sew a triangle to the base of each fleur, and then sew the fleurs together in pairs. Sew the pairs together to make the block centre.
4 Position and pin the quatrefoil fleur-de-lys to the background square. Line up the gold ovals and tuck them under the fleurs-de-lys, turning under the hem allowance between the fleurs but leaving the edges raw under the fleurs. Appliqué the ovals into position.
5 Finally, appliqué the quatrefoil fleur-de-lys, covering the raw edges of the ovals.

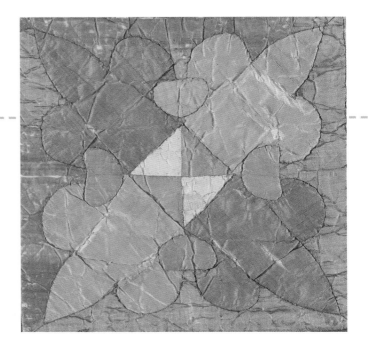

Fig 1
Whole block (25% size) – enlarge by 400%

Fig 1 shows the whole block reduced in scale and Fig 2 shows a quarter of the template at full size. Follow the instructions with the template.

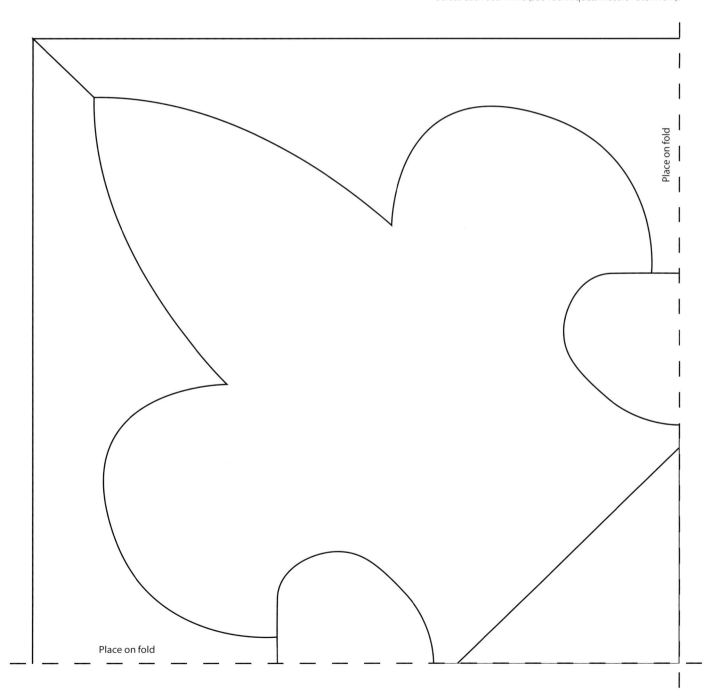

Fig 2
Template (quarter of design)
Actual size of whole template 13½in (34.3cm) square

Fold a 13½in (34.3cm) paper square into quarters and trace off the template, lining up along the folds as indicated by the dashed lines. Repeat the design for the three other quarters by tracing, or carefully cut out the pattern through all the layers with the paper still folded. Draw balance marks across each seam line (see Techniques: Mosaic Patchwork).

Place on fold

Place on fold

A quatrefoil fleur-de-lys with triangles centre

A target circle with hearts

Original patchwork blocks: 167, 174

Block size: 4½in (11.4cm) square finished

Original method: mosaic patchwork

Modern method: appliqué

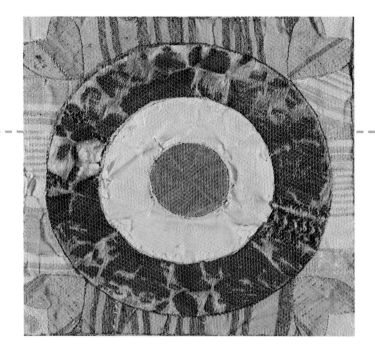

Original Method

1 Cut out and tack (baste) all pieces.
2 Sew the small corner pieces into the V of the hearts. Sew the hearts and border pieces together.
3 Insert the blue circle into the cream circle and insert this piece into the brown circle.
4 Finish the block by inserting the whole circle into the block border.

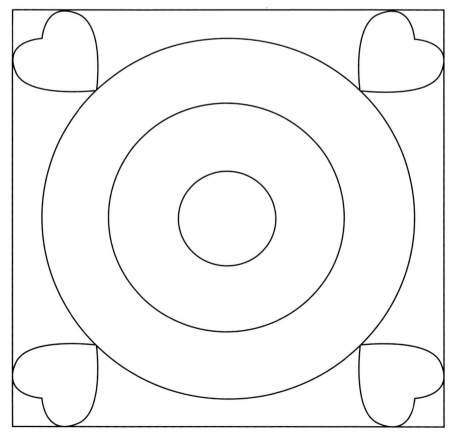

Modern Method

1 Cut one 5in (12.7cm) pale pink square for the block background – this will be visible at the block corners. Use the template to cut the four border pieces with an extra ¼in (6mm) allowance all round. Refer to Techniques: Appliqué for a choice of appliqué techniques. Position and pin these pieces.
2 Cut out the brown, cream and blue circles, adding an appropriate seam allowance for the technique you are using to the outside edge of each.
3 Align the brown circle and appliqué the outer edge. Repeat for the cream circle. Appliqué the blue circle to the block centre.
4 Arrange and appliqué the four hearts to finish.

Fig 1

Template

Actual size 4½in (11.4cm) square

This is the whole block at full size. Draw balance marks across each seam line (see Techniques: Mosaic Patchwork).

A pinwheel

Original patchwork blocks: 168, 173

Block size: 4½in (11.4cm) square finished

Original method: mosaic patchwork

Modern method: machine patchwork

Original Method

1 Cut out and tack (baste) all pieces.

2 Oversew the corner triangles together into squares and then sew the squares together to make the block. Match balance lines throughout the block.

Modern Method

1 Cut three 3⅛in (7.9cm) squares and cut them in half diagonally. Cut the yellow and blue stripes from a 2¼in (5.7cm) wide strip using one of the triangles from the template, so the stripes are on the bias. If you are using non-directional fabrics, cut four 3⅛in (7.9cm) squares instead, cutting each in half diagonally.

2 Machine sew the corner triangles together into squares and then sew the squares together to make the block.

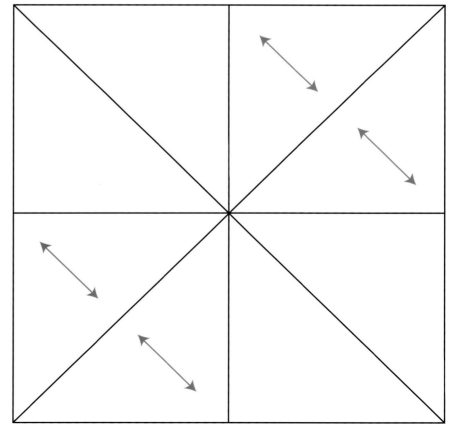

Fig 1
Template
Actual size 4½in (11.4cm) square

This is the whole block at full size. Arrows indicate fabric stripe directions. Draw balance marks across each seam line (see Techniques: Mosaic Patchwork).

A goose

Original patchwork blocks:
176, 180 (mirror image)

Block size: 9in x 13½in
(22.9cm x 34.3cm) finished

Original method:
mosaic patchwork

Modern method: appliqué

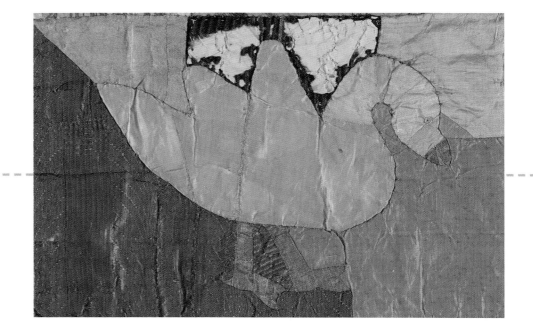

Original Method

1 Cut out and tack (baste) all pieces.
2 The goose body seams may be omitted,
as on the original coverlet they appear to
be recycling seams, otherwise begin by
oversewing the body pieces together.
3 Sew the two halves of the beak to the narrow
green background piece and then sew to the head.
4 Assemble the feet as follows. Sew the triangular
hind toe of each foot to the relevant blue
background piece and sew to the leg. Sew the
blue background piece underneath the feet.
5 Sew the leg section between the larger blue
background section and green background section.
6 Sew the upper background pieces together
in sequence. Now sew these to the top
of the bird, from the tail to the beak.
7 Sew the bottom half of the block to the
rest, starting at the top left corner and sewing
along the tail, breast and neck. Sew the seam
between the green and gold sections.
8 Embroider the eye to finish (see
Techniques: Embroidering Eyes).

Fig 1
Template
Whole block (25% size) – enlarge by 400%
Fig 1 shows the whole block reduced in scale and
Fig 2 shows the two parts of the template at full
size. Follow the instructions with the template.

The two geese blocks, mirror images of each other, are placed in a prominent position at the bottom of the coverlet, where they would have been very visible at the foot of the bed. The goose in original block 176 is all the same fabric, with seams that do not reflect the body shape, while this fabric has worn away in original block 180. The blue and brown stripe behind the geese may suggest water. Original block 180 has numerous recycling seams in the green background section. The template is taken from original block 176.

Modern Method

1 Cut a 9½in x 14in (24.1cm x 35.6cm) piece of green fabric for background. Use the template to cut the other background pieces with an extra ¼in (6mm) allowance all round. Cut the lower blue striped background pieces as one piece.

2 Turn under ¼in (6mm) where the gold upper corner piece overlaps the background fabric, leaving edges raw that will be under the goose body. Line up the edge of this piece with the block corner and appliqué.

3 Add the rest of the background pieces in the same way, turning under ¼in (6mm) to overlap the previous background piece each time. Turn under ¼in (6mm) at the foot for the final blue background piece.

4 Cut out the body, legs, and upper and lower beak, with appropriate seam allowances. The legs may each be cut in one piece. Pin the main part of the body in place. Line up and then appliqué the leg and beak sections.

5 Position the body to cover all the raw edges and then appliqué in place.

6 Embroider the eye to finish (see Techniques: Embroidering Eyes).

IDEA

The blue and brown striped fabric behind the goose may have been used by the maker of the coverlet to suggest water. It is one of two very similar wide blue and brown woven stripes used throughout the original coverlet. Similar stripes, in cotton, are sometimes used for shirting fabrics today, so you could look for something similar.

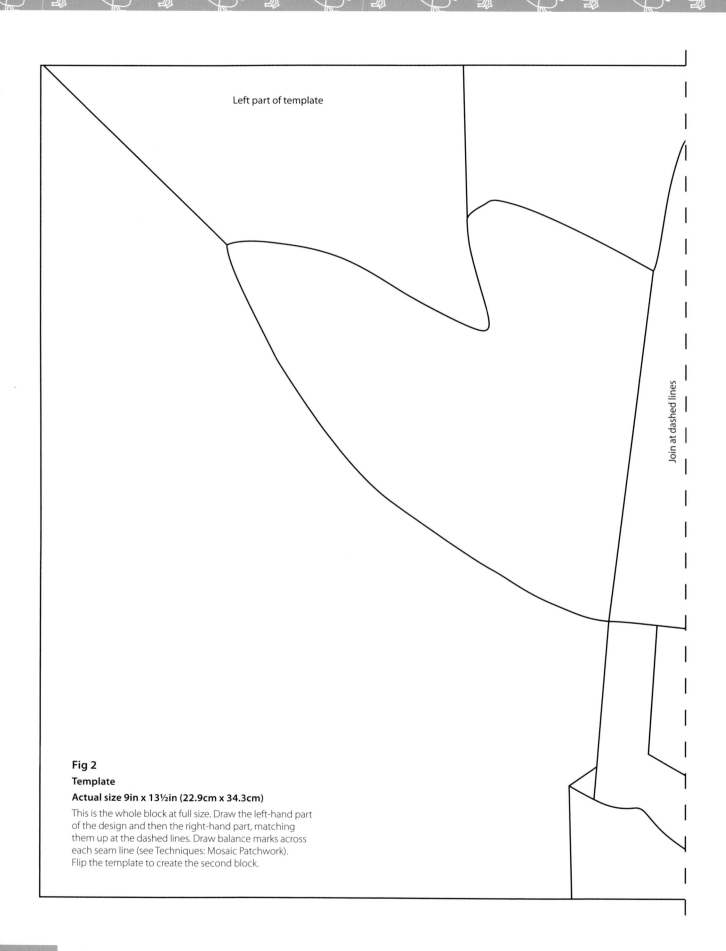

Left part of template

Join at dashed lines

Fig 2
Template
Actual size 9in x 13½in (22.9cm x 34.3cm)
This is the whole block at full size. Draw the left-hand part of the design and then the right-hand part, matching them up at the dashed lines. Draw balance marks across each seam line (see Techniques: Mosaic Patchwork). Flip the template to create the second block.

Right part of template

Join at dashed lines

An hourglass

Original patchwork blocks: 177, 179 (mirror image)

Block size: 4½in x 2¼in (11.4cm x 5.7cm) finished

Original method: mosaic patchwork

Modern method: appliqué

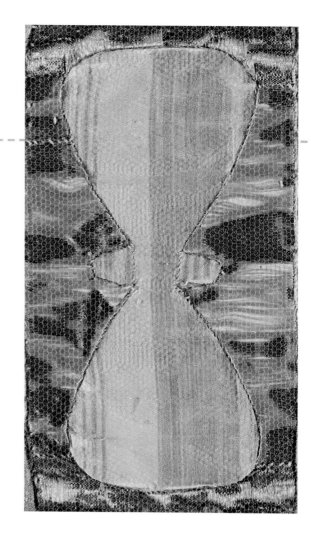

Original Method

1 Cut out and tack (baste) all pieces.

2 Sew the lugs of the hourglass to the background. Match balance lines throughout the block.

3 Assemble the various background pieces to frame the hourglass.

4 Insert the hourglass body into the background and sew all round to finish.

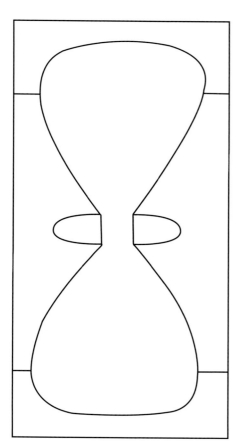

Modern Method

1 Cut one 5in x 2¾in (12.7cm x 7cm) piece for the background. Use the template to cut the hourglass from fabric, with appropriate seam allowances. Refer to Techniques: Appliqué for appliqué techniques.

2 Pin the hourglass to the background and position the lugs. Appliqué all the pieces, with the hourglass body covering the raw edges of the smaller pieces.

Fig 1
Template
Actual size 4½in x 2¼in (11.4cm x 5.7cm)
This is the whole block at full size.
Draw balance marks across each seam line
(see Techniques: Mosaic Patchwork).

This detail from the original coverlet shows the two rectangular hourglass blocks in position, with Pattern 68 (a trefoil with swag) between them.

A trefoil with swag

Original patchwork block: 178

Block size: 9in (22.9cm) square finished

Original method: mosaic patchwork

Modern method: machine patchwork and appliqué

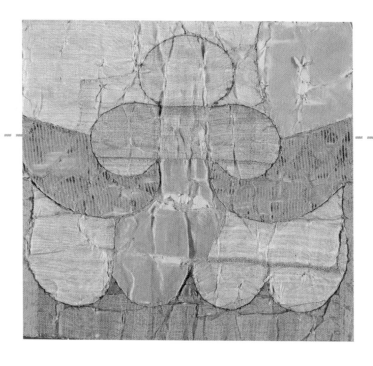

Original Method

1 Cut out and tack (baste) all pieces.

2 Construct the top of the trefoil and oversew to the swag first. Match balance lines throughout the block.

3 Sew the lower half of the swag to the lower half of the background. Sew the yellow striped side pieces to the upper background.

4 Sew the two halves of the block together, starting the sewing of the curves at the inner points and easing the curves together.

Modern Method

1 Cut a 9½in (24.1cm) light pink square for the background. Cut the yellow stripe and lower deep pink background pieces, adding ¼in (6mm) all round.

2 Turn under a ¼in (6mm) allowance on the top diagonal edge of each yellow striped piece and appliqué to the background. Add the lower pink section the same way, leaving raw the edges under the motif. Refer to Techniques: Appliqué for a choice of appliqué techniques, including needle-turn appliqué and freezer paper appliqué.

3 Cut out the trefoil swag motif, either seaming the top of the trefoil to the rest of the motif with a ¼in (6mm) seam, or cutting the whole motif in one piece. Add the appropriate turning allowance for your chosen appliqué technique.

4 Position and then appliqué the trefoil swag into place to finish the block.

Fig 1

Template

Whole block (25% size) – enlarge by 400%

Fig 1 shows the whole block reduced in scale and Fig 2 shows a half of the template at full size. Follow the instructions with the template.